THERE ARE NO
UNGUARDED MOMENTS

THERE ARE NO UNGUARDED MOMENTS

Bishop J. A. Tolbert 1st

authorHOUSE®

AuthorHouse™
1663 Liberty Drive
Bloomington, IN 47403
www.authorhouse.com
Phone: 1 (800) 839-8640

Published by AuthorHouse 06/15/2016

ISBN: 978-1-4918-3740-5 (sc)
ISBN: 978-1-4918-3739-9 (hc)
ISBN: 978-1-4918-3738-2 (e)

Library of Congress Control Number: 2013921323

Print information available on the last page.

Table of Contents

DEDICATION

Firstly, Rosemary, *"my Brown Sugar,"* the love of my life who consented to be my bride forty-nine years ago and loves me still, I honor with the writing of this book. Indeed, she is my inspiration for the love that shines forth in some of these stories. It is her eyes, smile and heart that gave me the fuel for the fire of love that burns in the stories about budding love. It is the wisdom of her mind and the sensitivity of her caring for others that provided the foundation for much of the understanding and good judgment that heals hurts. I have the pen of a ready writer in the crisis of these narratives because of the influence of her discernment and empathy that reaches into abysmal depths to bring forlorn and hopeless souls past their despair to a tomorrow where their future is bright and strong.

I dedicate this book secondly, to my four children whom I adore more than I love my life. Besides my own childhood experiences, these wonders of joy have provided me with fodder for so many of the ideas and storylines for this book. Each of them was unique from the others and brought to the banquet table of my life main entrees of learning experiences and condiments that perfectly seasoned those life lessons.

They also provided beverages of refreshing wit and topped it all off with delightful desserts of humor for my mind and abiding hope for my heart.

Thirdly, to my Church Family whom I have been privileged to serve as their Bishop, pastor, father (to some), brother and friend for the past thirty-seven years, I also dedicate this book. They have inspired me, encouraged me and given my life purpose in more ways than mere words can describe.

Fourthly, I wrote this work for all who feel that their lives are in the whimsical and capricious hands of chance. These hapless souls have not the revelation that our Father God is too loving and responsible to leave His Children unattended even for a nanosecond. For I realize that in the moment of that one billionth of a second, Satan could wreak more havoc in our lives than we could get out of in a lifetime.

Then, I have written to all those Children of God who have spent too much time living in suspense and too little time living in confidence because they felt all alone in their times of crisis.

Finally, this book is dedicated to my grandchildren who have either climbed into my lap as I dozed in my recliner and during *their busy times* interrupted *my quiet times* to say, "Gandy, please tell us one of your stories!" With these stories and more I have sought to entertain and teach life lessons to my grandchildren who are indeed God's gifts and promises to the future.

Preface

"SOMEBODY, PLEASE GET MY BACK!"

Because life is fraught with many unexpected occurrences, we who are wise buy such protection as medical, life, and accident insurances. We buy cars with air bags. We keep umbrellas in our cars. We purchase motorcycle helmets. Vitamin supplements are bought to prevent infections and disease and spare tires are commonly found in vehicles. These are just a few examples of the measures we take to prepare for and to prevent negative contingencies. There is no way, however, that we can be ready for all of the possible eventualities. Therefore, we depend on the best of all earthly protections - good friends!

Many Americans are fond of saying, "I've got your back". The meaning of this colloquialism is, "I'm protecting that part of your life that you cannot defend". God's Wisdom designed the body of man so that man's eyes cannot see to protect man's rear. Neither can man's arms and hands reach behind to the same extent that they can reach the front of man's body. So man often has itches that he cannot scratch and he has hurts in places that he cannot soothe.

It is noteworthy that true-born children of the King have no defenses that cover their backs. We don't have a posture for a good rearward defense. Our anterior defenselessness is divinely intended. God will never - in any situation - create a condition in man's life that causes man to feel that he doesn't need a divine savior and his spiritual family.

But God never wants His Body, His children to turn tail and run. Nor does the Captain of our souls want us to lay down our spiritual weapons and concede defeat. And why don't we have eyes that can see behind us? Why are we so unable to protect our backs? Why doesn't the Almighty God order the system of things so that no one can ever attack the hinder part of anybody else? He could simply never allow the thought of attacking the defenseless back to enter a person's mind.

Perhaps the primary reason is the Lord wanted every man to need every other man. He wanted mankind to provide for one another. It is clearly evident to this writer that God ordained that His entire creation exist in a symbioses relationship. For example, some birds live by eating the parasites that burrow into the backs of larger animals. The larger animals continue to live because the blood sucking bugs that could infect the larger animals with disease are eaten by the birds. So each creature's survival is dependent on the support and survival of the other.

Because no man can adequately watch his own back each should depend on his brother for this service. The result will be that there are no unprotected backs and "NO UNGUARDED MOMENTS!"

CHAPTER 1

"TRUST YOUR GOD TO BE YOUR GUARD"

When will Believers learn that God will not allow His children to suffer lost? As the Apostle, Paul, asserts, "I…am persuaded that he is able to keep that which I have committed unto me against that day." (II Tim. 1:12) (The all seeing eye of God is in every place beholding the good and the evil. Nothing can catch Him "off guard". God doesn't merely wait to see how life unfolds! Rather, God, as the Master Planner, Orchestrates the believer's life.

When the young man got up that morning he was so excited! He woke up praying and thanking God for taking complete control of his life. He asked his Savior to guide his footsteps and orchestrate his day.

Being thus armed, he jumped up from the bed and went straight to the dresser. There it was! My, how the sunlight danced through the facets of the beautiful three-carat, pear-shaped diamond engagement ring. It sparkled like liquid fire laced with millions of tiny glistening rainbows. When he picked it up, the diamond burst into a kaleidoscope of seemingly pulsating colors in the light of the morning sun that flooded through the bedroom window. He thought, "Oh, won't she be so happy when I ask her to marry me?" He knew she would say, "Yes".

It seemed that everything was going to be perfect that day. He quickly showered and dressed for work. He was so anxious to see her that he wondered how he would be able to survive the all day wait! He cooked and ate a quick breakfast and was out of the door in a flash.

Usually, he had a rush of adrenalin as he approached his pride and joy. The little car was five years old now but he had bought it when it was only three years old. For as long as he could remember he had wanted a car like this one. It was candy apple red with leather seats and shiny wood framing the dashboard. He still loved the way the dashboard lit up at night.

The little red sports car answered immediately when he turned the key in the ignition. Despite the wintry cold, he didn't even need to use the manual choke. He still loved the quiet rhythmic growl of the engine. The young man pushed the clutch in and eased the shift lever into first gear and started off to work.

When he got to work, on his desk was a note that said his supervisor wanted to see him as soon as he arrived. The young executive fought to hold down the fear that came over him. He knew that the company was cutting back on expenses and the employees with the least amount of seniority were being laid off first. Already three of his friends had been let go. He felt particularly sad for one of them; the one he had talked to about the love of God.

But he couldn't be laid off now when he needed all the money he could get! This would change everything! He couldn't ask the most wonderful girl in the world to marry him if he didn't have a job! Furthermore, he had prayed this morning that God would take charge of his day. Surely, God wouldn't, no - COULDN'T let this happen!

With a heart that fluctuated between fear and faith he knocked on the big oak door of the plush office of the vice-president in charge of marketing. Mr. Kingsley was a short, fat, heavy jowled man who was known to be the company's "hatchet man".

"Nobody ever gave me a break," he was known to say. His raspy voice growled, "Come in!" Entering, the young man could barely see the squat Buddha-like figure that blew constant billows of cigar smoke. The white smoke swirled past his large elephantine ears and circled around his loosed skinned bald head. His large bulbous red nose occasionally redirected the smoke toward whomever he talked to.

Mr. Kingsley peered through the fog of cigar smoke and looked the young man up and down for what seemed like a long minute. Finally, he said, "Son, as you know, the company is cutting back on the staff. What you don't know is that we are streamlining the work force for efficiency. Where we can, we are deleting positions and creating new positions that will be responsible for two to three of the former jobs. We have been watching you. We know that you don't have all the education that many of our young people in the company have. But for some reason we have decided that you have what it takes to handle one of these new positions. So, starting next Monday, you will have a substantial, a raise new office, a secretary and a new title. Congratulations, Son."

The young man could scarcely believe his ears. Only God could have put all of this together. The young man marveled at the way God had blessed him! "Sir, I won't let you down!" he promised. He couldn't get out of Mr. Kingsley's office fast enough to really thank the Lord for this wonderful blessing. Now he could not only afford the kind of honeymoon that he really wanted but he could even buy the house that he had looked at when all he could do was wish.

There is the day that the adversary attacks the life and love of the child of God. There is no need, though, for the <u>prepared</u> to despair. Let us learn that if we meet Jesus in the morning - we can meet anything and anybody all the day long.

Chapter 2

"THERE ARE NO UNGUARDED MOMENTS"

To the casual observer it may often seem that surely there is no authority that is in control. It may sometimes appear that either God is totally unaware of all that is going on in life or that God is a co-conspirator with the enemy to overthrow the Child of the King. For, all do not know that nothing can happen to the Blood Bought except God gives his permission! This understanding among the faithful is really a "no brainer".

What a confidence and an assurance the believer may walk in! Our Father will never allow His children to live for a moment without the benefit of His loving arms of protection.

One evening I was walking home from my job at Pete's Supermarket. I pulled my hat further down over my head and tightened the scarf around my neck in a vain effort to shield myself from the piercing, freezing wind. I hunched my shoulders forward as if to will my body to move ahead against the biting cold of one of the worse Michigan winters of my young life. Trying to ignore the cold that sliced into my shoes to numb my feet, I heard the cold North wind scream as if in harsh pain almost as if it cut itself on the sharp edges of the buildings that were downtown Detroit. I had greased my lips before I left home and was now hoping the Chap Stick would protect my trembling lips from splitting again today.

Despite the wintry weather, I followed my usual routine and paused beneath the old wooden shingle sign that old Doc Rivers so proudly hung above his door some thirty-five years ago. Again, I wondered how long the sign could last. I heard it creak and groan in tired protest against the unrelenting brutality of the howling winds. I was still watching when that old nail that had for a long time been pushing its way out of the shingle bracket - finally broke free. The wind seemed to me to be a co-conspirator with the nail as it blew a sudden and unexpected gust. And, with an unspoken cry of triumph, the blast quickly and easily relieved the nail of its seven-pound burden. Held to the building by only one hinge and thudding loudly against the building, the sign flapped in the wind like a pigeon with a broken wing. The nail was airlifted to the curb with a victorious "ping," where it bounced into the street to begin another adventure.

A silent presence was I in this mini drama. Above the insistent voice of the arctic-like gale, I heard the throaty roar of a fast approaching automobile. I could hear the downshifting of the transmission as the driver expertly executed a racing turn. The flashy little red sports car careened around the corner. The driver shifted into third gear and accelerated as he headed for the road that ran parallel to the Detroit River. The screech of his right tires was only faintly heard as the car fought a losing battle with the gravitational pull known as centrifugal force. Fighting to get a grip on the blacktop, the right front tire of the car found the nail. The air jet streamed out of the tire with a "Woosh!" For a brief moment I saw fear twist the face of the young driver as he fought to regain control of the vehicle that was bucking and fighting against his will. The squalling wind emitted a high pitched wail of clashing tones. For a quick moment it seemed that it was cheering for either the car or the force of gravity that threatened the driver with certain death. I couldn't tell which!

The flat tire threw the entire car off balance. It went into a swerving skid and finally slid along a guardrail. The driver braked hard, downshifting with a skill that was born of years of practice. Still, he crashed side-long into the guard rail. Though everything happened at lightning speed, I saw it in slow motion as if watching a movie frame by frame. As I watched, enthralled, it appeared that the car and the guardrail were locked in a morbid and deadly dance. The discord and the awful disharmony of metal against unyielding metal gave rise to the notion that the little red sports car and the guard rail were providing their own music for the dance - a kind of unmusical heavy metal music - loud and so off key! The guardrail bent and twisted under the impact that left a smear of red paint along the rail. The little red sports car appeared to mark the guardrail with blood as if from a gash in its side. The guardrail seemed determined to be faithful to its duty though the blood-red paint swathe and the dent in the guardrail threatened that the little car would not survive this crash. I marveled as the guard rail refused to give in and allow the car to plunge into the cold black waters of the Detroit River. The driver huddled over the steering wheel shivering in fear and crying tears of relief as he praised God for the integrity of the guardrail that spared his life.

Isn't God's timing wonderfully on point? How beautiful are the words of promise that are found in the book of Isaiah, "And it shall come to pass, <u>that before they call, I will answer;</u> and while they are yet speaking, I will hear." (Isa 65:24 KJV) Someone planned the safety of the guardrails years before they were needed by this driver. The Greater Watcher provided for this day; for this moment; for this driver by inspiring someone to install this highway "safety net" and because this was faithfully done this man lived to drive anther day!

CHAPTER 3

THE CARING SHADOW

Human beings are so often so unmindful of their own frailty in the light of their own assessment and analysis of their strengths and abilities. And though a sense of individualism and a quality of self-assurance, when well placed, are hard to beat, the wise person will know when aid and assistance is warranted. But for the times when one is reaching beyond one's ability to grasp or putting a weight of responsibility upon oneself that is unreasonable there is most definitely a grave need for the vigilance of a faithful Watcher.

It was a warm and sunny autumn morning. The morning sounds were filling the air. The blue jays were fussing at the crimson cardinals outside the window. The robins and the sparrows were chirping their praise at such a picture perfect day. The two squirrels that made their home in the big pecan tree in the back yard were chasing one another around the yard and from tree to tree. I remember that the yard always seemed to grow larger as I mowed it.

Inside the sprawling brick, ranch style house on Wren road in the Bird Creek addition of Temple, Texas, my little five-year old son, Shawn, was eating breakfast. He was going to start his third day at Cater Elementary School. His eyes were all aglow and his baby "afro" was freshly combed. He really looked like he had something on his mind as he used his fork to push his food around on his plate. I could tell that Shawn had something on his mind.

"Okay, Shawn, what are you thinking about now?" I asked. It was not unusual for Shawn to come up with a doozy of a question or statement. Shawn looked up from his Sugar Frosted flakes and surprised everyone by announcing, "I don't want anybody to walk me to school anymore. I'm a big boy now. I'm not a baby! The other kids don't have their father or mother walking them to school."

Now, we only lived one block from his elementary school. But Shawn was so small and so helpless! Sure, he knew the way to school but he was our baby boy! My wife and I looked at each other. Neither of us was willing to let go of our baby and accept that he was able to face this world alone. We knew, though, that among his friends he must stand as an equal.

So our question was, "Do we let our little boy (who now seems so much smaller than he did a few minutes ago) walk by himself and take a chance on something happening to him? Or do we just not let the way his friends look at him be such a big deal to us?

As I looked at Shawn, I felt so proud of him. Shawn had just taken the first of many steps in a kind of urban rite of passage that would eventually and ultimately enter him into manhood. I also felt the fear of a father who knows all too well that there is a big, cold and mean world out there.

Shawn was gazing back at me with great confidence in his eyes when I said to him, "All right, son, I know you are a big boy now. You go ahead. I won't walk with you to school anymore."

He seemed to swell with a new found strength. He got up from the table and picked up his lunch box (he always wanted to take his lunch and enjoy all the goodies that his mother prepared for him). He squared his shoulders back and looking very much like the little man that he was he hitched up his pants, kissed his mother, gave me a hug and headed out the door.

I watched through the kitchen window as he went out the back gate. I let him get just out of the yard and head down the street before I went out the back door after him. I eased the gate open and sidled up behind the big pecan tree that was by the gate. I saw him walking down the street swinging his lunch box and humming the song to the He-Man cartoon. He never even looked back! I hid behind trees and cars all the way to Cater Elementary school. I was careful not to take a chance on being caught but I had to stay close enough to him to reach him quickly should the need arise.

Every day after that for a long time I followed Shawn to school until I knew that he was not just brave enough to go by himself but was really old enough. Until now Shawn never knew that I was his "Caring Shadow."

To watch Shawn was not only an act that had its origin in the heart of love, it was the only thing that I could do, for I am his watcher. My call to be his watcher was not simply self-proclaimed. His love for me does not allow me to be less than his guardian. I never have been satisfied knowing that my son was unprotected. My reward for watching Shawn was the peace and the assurance that Shawn was safe. True love always calls the lover to the privilege and responsibility watching.

CHAPTER 4

IN KITTY WHEN DEATH IS INEVITABLE

What do you do when you have lived enough life to know beyond the shadow of doubt the reality that, at some time, under some conditions and in some places – death is inexorable; death is inescapable? When you have been on the receiving end of Death's bludgeon and have reeled and rocked in the throes of your unrelenting grief - the choices are simple! Either you surrender to the belief that the certainty of death is so that you must concede to its unavoidable end or you rest in the knowledge that the One Who has power over life and death is on your side! If you choose the latter option, you then relax in complete security knowing that Jesus is going to stay up all night and there is no use in both of you losing your sleep!

CHAPTER 5

"CAN YOU TRUST YOUR WATCHER?"

Sometimes it is necessary to watch your "watcher. I know that hardly seems to be the order of the day but if your watchers need watching - WATCH 'EM! Then, there are those "fair weather friends" who promised to stand with you and did - until the going got tough! Some watchers may watch for themselves first. In this case one may find that the whole purpose of having a watcher is made a mockery.

The Posse was there! Junebug, Wobbles, Spider and Ricky Stevenson were sitting in the shade of the fire escape tunnel at the Duffield elementary school. Peewee was there too. He wasn't really in The Posse because he was too young. You had to be a least ten years old to be in The Posse. Peewee was allowed to run with the Posse because he was Junebug's kid brother. My name is Buddy. I'm twelve years old.

We were on summer vacation and this was one of those days when there was nothin' to do and nobody felt like doin' nothin' anyway. So, feelin' kinda lazy, we were lookin' up at the clouds and makin' pictures in the sky.

"Man, you guys must be blind! Cain't you see that stallion rarin' up?" I said. "It's right there in front of you!" For the last five minutes I had been trying to show the fellas the wildest, most beautiful stallion I had ever seen. Its long tail reached all the way down to its back feet. Its eyes were wide open and alert. I could almost hear the great horse snortin' with his nostrils flarin'. And in my mind's eye I saw the great horse's tail whipping back and forth like a bed sheet on Mamma's clothes line on a windy day. I could see the muscles in his chest bulging out and promising the strength and speed of the fastest horse that had ever ridden the sky winds. The guys just couldn't see it though. But I guess I love horses so much that I seemed to see 'em everywhere.

"Thoot, I'm tired of thith anyway! Leth do thumthin' elth," whined seven-year-old Peewee with a sniff. Now, you've got to understand a couple things about Peewee. First, his two front teeth came out real early. They probably came out so soon because he was always eatin' his favorite candies, Blackjacks, and Mary Jane. Anyway, he always pronounced the letter "S" with a "th".

The second thing about Peewee is that he always seemed to have a cold and a runny nose. In the summer he had a cold. In the fall, winter and spring, *Peewee had a cold*! He was always sniffing and wiping his nose on his shirt's sleeve and on the backs of his hands. I guess there is an advantage to his being so germy though. He never had to share his apple, his Dairy Cream cone or any food. I mean, it seemed that you could just see germs crawling over anything he touched.

"Hey, Peewee, I sure could use some of those big juicy looking cherries we saw yesterday!" Junebug, Peewee's older brother, piped up.

"Man, where'd you guys see some cherries yesterday?" Wobbles asked. Wobbles was always looking for something to eat. As a matter of fact, that's why we called him, "Wobbles". He was so fat that he wobbled when he walked. Wobbles was the laziest member of the posse but when there was even the smallest chance that he could get something to eat Wobbles really got busy. Already he was lickin' his lips and swallowing and imagining how those cherries would taste.

"Over in mean old Mith Pickle'th back yard," Peewee answered. We wath walkin' down the alley kickin' a can on our way home from Laurie Brotherth Thuper market and I kicked that can right through a hole in old Mith Pickle's fenth and it got thtuck in her hedgeth. When I went to get it I looked up and thaw the reddeth, biggeth, juithieth cherryth I ever thaw and they were juth callin' me to come and get 'em!"

"Yeah, but y'all know mean old Miz Pickles! She ain't goin' to give us nothin'!" Ricky reminded everybody. "Man, *she's just plain mean!*"

The truth is that not one of us really knew Miz Pickles. We were all goin' by what we thought was the truth. And that was based on what we'd heard about her. Our truth about Miz Pickles was about as correct as if each of us tried to set our watches by one another's watch and nobody had the correct time in the first place.

Her name really was "Mrs. Pickrell." But the posse called her, "Mean Old Miz Pickles". Nobody knew where we heard it first but we all knew that Miz Pickles was a mean old witch who could just wave her hand at you and stiffen your tongue up so you'd never talk again. Also, we knew that she could just look at you with those strange, green eyes and you would lose weight and just shrivel up like a prune before the next morning. And there wasn't any medicine or operation that could help you. Besides that, she was the stingiest old woman in town (at least that's what the Posse all agreed that we had heard).

Then there was something that we never talked about above a whisper. We knew that Mean Old Miz Pickle has *a little girl that she stole away from her mother and father*! And, she keeps that little girl locked up all day long and only lets her out at night. Junebug even told us how he was walkin' down the alley behind Mean Old Miz Pickle's house with his uncle one night and he heard a little girl singing all by herself. His uncle was too busy thinkin' like grown folks do and seemed like he never heard the little voice at all. Junebug said that he couldn't help but walk faster. He kept lookin' over his shoulder all the way home.

The first time we talked about the little girl we all bragged about what we would do and how we would help her escape if we ever got the chance. We all agreed that the reason we were duty bound to save her was, "Cause, bein' a kid, she is one of our own - even if she is only a girl."

"I've got it!" I exclaimed all of a sudden, "Since Peewee is smaller than the rest of us he can just watch out for Mean Old Miz Pickles while we climb the Cherry tree and get the cherries! And we'll just give him some of ours so he'll have as much as all of us."

"Yeah, Peewee, how 'bout it?" Wobbles said. "I can't wait to sink my teeth into some of them cherries!"

"Okay, if ya'll will guarantee that old greedy gut, Wobbleth ith going to thare with me too!" Peewee bargained.

Everybody knew that *Wobbles didn't get up off of no food for nobody!*

"If he don't we'll take all of his from him and give 'em to you!" I promised.

So, we took off down the street to get some free brown paper bags from Laurie Bros. Super market to put our cherries in. Then we headed to Mrs. Pickrell's house.

We told Peewee to stand guard in the yard right by the gate to the alley where he could see Mrs. Pickrell's back door and the Cherry tree. Then everybody scampered up the Cherry tree; everybody except Wobbles, that is. He crawled, climbed, panted and complained himself up the tree. Finally, everyone was settled in the tree. Because I was greedy and skinny enough, I climbed to the top branches; higher than the rest of the guys 'cause that's where the best cherries were.

Well, we were eatin' as much as we were baggin' so we never noticed when Peewee's eyes nearly popped out of his head! He'd heard the creaky old hinges when Miz Pickrell opened the back screen door. He realized that the first person she was goin' to see was him! All of the stories that he knew about what she did to little kids just ran around, climbin' over one another in his head and little Peewee panicked big time! He never decided to run! It just happened! He didn't want to be the next little kid Mean Old Miz Pickle stole! And he sure didn't want his tongue to stiffin' up so he couldn't ever talk again. But what he was most scared of was that she might look at him with those strange green eyes and make him shrivel up by in the morning and no medicine and no doctor could make him better. So, he didn't take the chance that she would hear the creaky old fence. He just slipped out through a hole in the fence and cut out for home as fast as his little legs could carry him.

Miz Pickrell had been in her kitchen washing some greens she was goin' to cook for dinner when she thought she heard some noise in the backyard. Wiping her hands on her apron, she cocked her head to the side and muttered to herself, "Seems like somebody's in my Cherry tree."

She opened the screen door and stepped out on the porch. Shielding her eyes from the sun with her hand, she said, "Lawd, some kids is in my Cherry tree again! One of these days one of 'em is goin' to fall and break his neck! Why cain't they see there's danger in climbin' that tree?"

About that time, Wobbles spotted her. "Hey Guys! It's Mean Old Miz Pickles!" He wasn't far up in the tree so he just half jumped and half fell down and wobbled across the yard as fast as he could! One by one we all climbed and jumped down like so many squirrels. Everybody made it before Miz Pickrell could get to the tree - except me! I was so high that I couldn't get down fast enough! Plus, my suspenders kept gettin' snagged on the branches. By the time I got down, you guessed it, Mean Old Miz Pickrell was waitin' for me! As soon as I hit the ground she had me! She grabbed me by my right ear and yanked it!

"Why is you stealin' my cherries, Buddy? I know yo' mamma and she's a church goin', God fearin' lady. And yo' daddy is a preacher! You oughta be an example to those other kids. All y'all had to do was asked me and y'all could have had them cherries and used my ladder to git em instead of y'all riskin' yo' necks like that."

Every time she spoke a word loudly she yanked my right ear like she was surely going to tear it right off! I had to tiptoe to lessen the pain! I half walked and half jumped all the way home with my head cocked to one side.

Miz Pickrell yanked and scolded and scolded and yanked all the way to my house where she told my mother the whole story.

I not only got a spanking. I had to stay in my room for the rest of the week with no TV 'cause my Mom said I was stealin' like a "common thief!" I didn't even know that there were different kinds of them!

The fallacy with having anyone other than the Savior, Jesus Christ for the primary Watcher is that only Jesus can be expected to always Watch for everything. He is the only One who cannot be bought, intimidated, tricked nor conned into Watching. If He had been the Watcher He would have made the kids understand that they must not steal the cherries in the first place! The true Watcher does not watch only after the fact but he watches before one ever gets into calamity. Such is the nature of the Master Watcher.

CHAPTER 6

MANDY JO, THE WOUNDED HEALER

"A good name is rather to be chosen than great riches…" Prov. 22:1 KJV

You have tried hard to earn the kind of reputation that defines you as honest, noble, generous, kind, loving and indeed having a character that is of the highest order! Yet, you find that those very same most excellent elements of your character worked in concert to deliver you into the hands of folk who would rather gossip about things they don't understand than to learn the laudable truths about you! They talk about you as it they are experts on YOU! They give their opinions of you as matters of FACTS! And you have to live with their misguided truths!

It was late one night in the city of Detroit, Michigan. Actually, about thirty minutes before Laurie Bros. Super Market was to close. It closed at ten o' clock during the week. My name is Buddy Tolbert. I am twelve years old and I am the best speller in my class. I am also the fastest and most expressive reader (that's what my teacher, Mrs. Sherman, said - not me).

Our mother asked if anybody wanted some ice cream and all seven of her children answered in no uncertain terms, "Yippee!" I was next to the oldest of my brothers and sisters. So, because my older brother was still doing' his homework, I had to go to the store to get the ice cream.

I knew that the sooner I got back the sooner we could eat ice cream so I decided to take a short cut through the alley between Dubois Street and Monroe. I cut through the alley and saw a dim light in Mean Ole Miz Pickle's backyard (her name really was Miss Pickrell but all the kids called her "Mean Ole Miz Pickles").

I was really haulin' it down the alley. All I could hear were my own footsteps and my own breathin'. While I ran, I liked to listen to my foot steps on the concrete alley. I was pretending that I was an Apache brave who was running to take a message to our war chief (I always made up stories and I was the star in all of them). This night I had to take the message to our war chief not to attack the neighboring tribe because what we thought was a problem between our tribes was only an unfortunate misunderstanding.

I was enjoying the staccato sound of my footsteps on the concrete alley when I heard a sound that didn't belong to the night. It didn't belong to the alley either. I slowed to a trot and heard the sweetest little voice singing "Amazin' Grace". I came to a complete stop right by Mean Ole Miz Pickel's backyard. I looked through the hedges and through the fence and saw a pretty dark haired girl about twelve years old sitting in the old homemade swing that hung from Miss Pickle's cherry tree.

All of the kids in the neighborhood had wondered and even offered suggestions as to why old Miss Pickles had a swing in her tree. We knew it wasn't for herself! Somehow, the story that most of us believed was that "Mean Ole Miz Pickles had stolen a little girl from her parents and kept her locked up in the house and only let her go out at night.

I looked at the little girl and even in the silvery moonlight I could tell that she had the palest skin color I had ever seen (and I knew that it wasn't because of the moonlight). I couldn't take my eyes off of her! Her hair was so wavy and silky looking. She had on a little suit that looked dark blue in the moonlight. It had a large white collar and little red buttons. She even wore a little blue and white hat with a red ribbon that streamed out behind her as she tried to pump herself higher and higher still on the swing. Her white gloves looked so clean as she hung on to the rope of the swing. I couldn't help noticing that she had on some white knee- high socks that made her little blue shoes look so shiny! Actually, she looked like she was on her way to church!

I wondered who she was 'cause I had never seen her before. I mean, if she was new to the neighborhood somebody would have seen her move in and the word would certainly have gotten around. Seein' as how I was the leader of our Posse (western shows were popular on the TV back in those days so that was what me and all of the fellas in the neighborhood called ourselves – the Posse). There was no way that this little girl could have moved in without somebody noticin' and whoever discovered her was bound to let me know.

Then, like a streak of lightnin' out of the blue it hit me! This was the little girl we had all heard about! This was the little girl that Mean Ole Miz Pickles had stole from her parents! We had all heard about her but I was the first one to see her up close! So I watched her and watched her. Her voice was the voice of an angel and her song touched me like nothin' had ever touched me before. As I looked at the scene before me I saw the porch that was almost as long as the entire rear of the house and was lit up by the yellow light that hung from the ceiling. I saw the big cherry tree that extended one of its great branches over to the side of the porch and the swing that hung from the thickest branch. But what really got my attention was the little girl that was dressed up in a beautiful suit, shiny shoes, white gloves and hat and was sittin' on a swing singin' Amazin' Grace.

What struck me the most was - *how happy she looked!* She didn't look like no girl that had been stole from her family!

I don't know how long I had watched her - maybe five minutes, maybe more, maybe less. But all of a sudden she stopped singing, jumped off the swing and ran straight at me before I had a chance to get away. She looked right into my face and said in the cutest little high pitched voice, "It ain't nice to spy on people."

I didn't know what to say. "I... I... I ain't spyin' on nobody," I stammered.

"Well, what do you call it when you peek through somebody's hedges and watch 'em and never even say "Hey"? What's your name anyhow?"

"Buddy Tolbert", he replied. "What's yours?"

"Mandy Jo and I live here. You live over on Clinton Street."

"How do you know where I live?" I asked in surprise.

"My grandmommy drives me around at night and sometimes I see you and your brothers and sisters out on the porch or sittin' on the curb under the street light in front of your house. I wish I could play with you but I can't. My grandmommy won't let me."

"Why?" I asked in surprise. "You mean that mean old witch, Miz Pickles really did steal you away from your family and keeps you locked up in the house all day long and won't let you out until the night time?" I blurted out.

"Don't you call my grandmommy no witch and her name is Miss Pickrell, Buddy Tolbert! P-I-C-K-R-E-L-L! And SHE AIN'T NO WITCH!" she shouted at me. "She is the nicest, sweetest, kindest lady in the world! And I oughta know! Didn't she take me in and raise me and feed me and buy me clothes since my daddy and my momma died in a car wreck when I was three years old? So, don't you say those mean things about my grandmommy ever again! And anyway, if it's any of your business, Mr. Nosy, my Grandmommy loves me!

All of a sudden I was afraid that her shoutin' at me would surely bring Ole Miz Pickles to the backdoor to see what was goin' on. But just then the little angry angel started talkin' quieter.

"Why she don't let me go out in the day time is - I've got skin cancer. And the sun makes my cancer grow faster so I stay in the house all day and only come out at night. My grandmommy loves me enough to make me stay in the house when I want to go out and play with you and your friends. Like the other day when y'all were stealin' our cherries. I saw y'all when y'all first came into our yard. I wanted to run out and play then but I knew y'all would get into trouble. And besides, Grandmommy wouldn't have let me go outside in the sun 'cause she loves me and wants me to live as long as I can."

I was so surprised first at her outburst and then at what she said that I couldn't think of anything to say in my defense. So I just said, "Why are you wearing' those Sunday clothes tonight?"

"This is Saturday night. And on Saturday night my grandmommy brushes my hair 'til it shines. "'Til it shines like a black diamond in the night" is what my Grandmommy says. I ain't never seen no black diamond but I 'magine it's the blackest black you ever saw! Every Saturday night my Grandmommy lets me dress up. And I pretend that I'm goin' to go to church with everybody else. But I know that I never will go back to church 'cause most people ain't got no good manners. I don't want everybody starin' at me and pointin' and whisperin' behind my back and feelin' sorry for me 'cause I look different. But, it's me that decided not to go to church - not my Grandmommy."

Again, I didn't know what to say. So I just said, "Can I come over and swing some nights?"

"I would really like that 'cause I ain't never had no friend before," Mandy Jo said. "But only if you don't tell everybody about me and my skin cancer."

"I promise," I said. "I won't tell anybody but my Mamma. 'Cause I know she'll care and pray for you."

I never did get the ice cream that night but when I told my Momma the reason she never got even a little bit upset with me. She really understood! She even let me go over to Mandy Jo's house two to three times a week that summer. And I played with her in the moonlight.

Sometimes, she was too tired to play so I just pushed her gently in the swing. She wasn't even heavy.

Lots of times we didn't even talk much. We just sat on the steps and thought. I used to wonder what she was thinking 'bout. But I never asked her 'cause I knew if she wanted to - she would tell me. She was like that. She was the most honest person I ever knew. Seems like she knew that she could trust me with anything she wanted to tell me. Only twelve! But she seemed so many years older than I thought I would ever be.

I knew from the first night that *I would never forget that summer!* I always felt that I grew up in my thinking more that summer than any time in my life up to that time and Mandy Jo taught me. Mandy Jo was the wisest little girl I knew. Maybe she was able to learn so much about life so fast 'cause she knew she didn't have much time to study life. She taught me to feel some of what people were feelin' and not to have to ask so many questions. She also taught me to appreciate the quiet breathing time between sentences. I even learned that sometimes the solutions are not as important as just thinking about the problems. I even figured out that there are times when the answers are just plain unnecessary.

I got to know Miss Pickrell that summer. I thought that she really was "the nicest kindest lady in the world" (besides my Momma).

I never said "Goodbye" to Mandy Jo because I never really wanted to leave her. I knew that she was very sick and I always thought that saying "Goodbye" might somehow make her die sooner. I was always afraid that she would be gone before I got back.

Somehow, at the end of that summer, I knew that I would never forget her. I grew to love Mandy Jo and I miss her still after all of these years. And I always like to remember that I was the only best friend she ever had.

Miss Pickrell was as selfless as she was faithful to her twelve years old charge. The cost to her reputation was never as important as was her responsibility to her granddaughter. Her love for Mandy Jo was a fulfilling and satisfying portion.

Such is the life of the true watcher. Though everyone else misunderstood Mrs. Pickrell, the Watcher - she understood why she watched! And that is all that mattered.

CHAPTER 7

THE ANATOMY OF A "WATCHER"

As sure as t14here are rewards and benefits that are derived from being a faithful and dutiful "Watcher," so it is that, more often than not, there are often costs of grave consequences to be borne by the "Watcher!" Because your love will not allow you to do less than pay the prices that are demanded by your "Watch," oft times all you can do is find comfort in the promise and admonishment of King David when he said, "Wait on the Lord: be of good courage, and he shall strengthen thine heart: wait, I say, on the Lord." Ps 27:14-28:1 KJV

The two-bedroom clapboard house had a more than ample kitchen and a modest living room. The features she liked best were the fireplace with the wide mantle and the front porch with the roof over it. There was nothing she liked more than sitting in her living room on a cold wintry evening with a roaring fire snapping and crackling in the fireplace. She truly loved the toasty fire and its cozy warmth. The subtle smell of the hickory logs burning and the soft glowing colors that bathed the room in their shadowy light somehow relaxed her and comforted her in ways that few things could. The whole scene made looking into the past and seeing what used to be - such a friendly and consoling experience. At her age, most of the pictures she saw in her mind's eye, even those of joyous events, caused her a sadness that she knew had its beginning in the heart of nostalgia. Few people seem to understand the need the aged have for consolation when they must constantly look forward to a future that can never be and see it pale in the shadow of what can never be again. But the genial luminescence of the fireplace made the pictures on the mantle seem to come alive. Sometimes, the moving fingers of shadows on the wall from the firelight seemed to distort things in the room. At times, she could almost believe that her Roy winked at her from his picture on the mantle, in the glow of the fire's gentle radiance.

She also loved to sit on the porch in the early mornings and watch the children swinging their lunch pails and playing on their way to school. She enjoyed the sing song sound of their sometimes dissonant voices. Though the notion may be a classic oxymoron, it is nevertheless the truth that the children's discordant voices were always harmonious to her.

Moreover, watching the young ones was like watching fish in an aquarium. Something was always happening and there was no way one could predict what the children would do next. One moment they were just walking along the sidewalk and the next moment they were chasing one another. One moment they were chasing one another and the next they were throwing rocks at birds or clacking sticks that they rubbed on the picket fences while they skipped along the sidewalk and so on.

On the mantle over the fireplace were three pictures. One showed her daughter and her husband on their wedding day. Whenever she spoke of that picture she said, "On that day the good Lord must surely have come to the wedding. I know that He and some of His beautiful angels (you know they really like weddings in Heaven) were sitting in Heaven's throne room looking down on the whole glorious affair. And my, but that was a wedding to make the Lord want to hurry and marry His church!"

There was also a picture of her daughter, her son-in-law and their one-year old daughter, Mandy Jo. The kindly old grandmother remembered the day her daughter gave her that picture. Her daughter and her son-in-law had gone to the park. They had taken her granddaughter there to show her the ducks and the swans in the pond. A man was there who said he was a grandfather and he had been painting a watercolor of that beautiful spring morning. He had seen them taking pictures of little Mandy Jo and offered to take one of the whole family. In the picture, Mandy Jo was sitting on her mother's lap on a swing that was near the pond and her daddy was standing behind them. The smiles on their faces gave no hint of the terrible life changing tragedy that would soon – much too soon – change their family forever.

The third photograph was of her husband, Roy. It was taken after he had graduated from boot camp when he was in the Marines. The young face that looked back at her had eyes that were filled with love and commitment, devotion and loyalty, promise and anticipation of life. He had shared grand ideas with her of what their lives were to be after the war. In all these years no one had ever made her feel like she did when she looked into those eyes. It was over forty years ago and how she missed him still!

On the date of their wedding anniversary and on his birthday, she wept for him. On Valentine's Day and Christmas, she also lamented his passing. And on the anniversary of his death - she still shed briny tears for her loneliness but she also shed happy tears for the joy of having known him. Most of all she was so grateful for having been so loved, so cherished, by her Roy.

Mrs. Mona Pickrell never expected that such great satisfaction would come from taking her granddaughter into her home after her parents were killed. But since Mandy Jo arrived, her heart had been filled with more joy than she ever knew was possible. She found that Mandy Jo was really a morning baby. She seemed to wake up every morning as the gentle rays of the sun quietly peeked through the gossamer curtains and warmed her soft walnut skin. For Mandy Jo, a giggle or a gurgle always seemed to be just on the tip of her lips. Mrs. Pickrell always loved the way there was music in Mandy Jo's laughter. A great comfort she was to her grandmother during the dark days of her grieving. Mrs. Pickrell knew that without Mandy Jo her time of sadness would have been so much longer and harder to bear.

Just when she had finally come to terms with the deaths of her daughter and son-law, Mandy Jo got sick. She had been sick before with colds in the winter, chicken pox when she turned three and even the measles when she was five. But Mrs. Pickrell knew from the beginning of the illness that this sickness was the worse Mandy Jo had ever had.

After much testing at the county hospital, the diagnosis was made. Mandy Jo was slowly dying of skin cancer! Mrs. Pickrell always trusted God but to have contentment in this tragedy was totally beyond any rationale that she could afford. Without her consent, the questions kept nagging her with demands for a relief that she felt could only come with knowing the answers. The questions that bothered her were, "Why?" and "Why Mandy Jo?" "Why must I lose my granddaughter after losing both her parents (and her mother was my only child)?" None of this made any sense. Mrs. Pickrell had even lost her husband in World War Two when they were young and so much in love! For a while, Mrs. Pickrell felt that all she knew how to do was lose and suffer her losses. Now, Mandy Jo and she were all that were left of their family.

Mrs. Pickrell was sitting on her porch. Today she could not control her thoughts. She just kept thinking about her daughter and son-in-law. It was Tuesday and for the entire year Mrs. Pickrell kept expecting her daughter to drive up in front of the house. She always came over on Tuesdays for spaghetti. Except that - *she never came anymore*!

"How sad it is for a mother to outlive her children!" Mrs. Pickrell soliloquized. "My hopes for a more fulfilling life were in my child. I expected that through her reach I would lay hold on things that were only dreams to me. There are joys that I never knew nor spent time seeking to know because I was too busy. I had to make my ends meet. And many times all my ends didn't seem to even live in the same neighborhood."

For much of her life, troubles with death and sickness seem to press Mrs. Pickrell beyond measure and she never knew the

"Why" of it all. But what she sometimes found more hurtful to bear is the fact that no one seemed to understand her and the choices she had been forced to make.

Many decisions were made because her love always seemed to have a mind of its own. Mrs. Pickrell couldn't do lest nor differently than her love for her granddaughter required.

She took Mandy Jo to church from the time that she first came to live with her. Mandy Jo was sick even then. She was six years old when she was diagnosed with skin cancer. The doctors advised that she not be taken out into the sun. The sun would speed the growth of the cancer and further shorten her all too short life span. Mrs. Pickrell started right away keeping Mandy Jo in the house during the day - out of the sun. Mandy Jo had such delicate skin! Mrs. Pickrell didn't realize how pale Mandy Jo would get from not being in the sun. It wasn't until they went to church one evening that she was made aware that Mandy Jo's skin had changed from walnut brown to a very pale brownish-gray color.

Quite often the life of the "Watcher" is altered by necessities brought about because of the special needs of the one who is "Watched." These sacrifices are not grievous or dreadful to the "Watcher" because they are simply the way things have to be for the treasure that is being provided for and guarded. It is not unlikely that the "Watcher" will receive as much as the "Watcher" gives to the "Watching" process! There is a heightened sensitivity to the needs of others and an increase in patience for them. There is also an enhanced appreciation of the Watcher's own frailty and mortality that causes the "Watcher" to walk more circumspectly, honoring every moment of life! The true "Watcher" may be found so close to the prevailing issue that changes in the scenario may escape notice. The things that are of paramount importance are the safety, wellbeing and the quality of life of the one being "Watched."

CHAPTER 8

THE WOUNDED HEALER

Our Omniscient, Omnipotent and Omnipresent God is so vast in his range and so Mighty in His Power and He is so Understanding in his assessments that He rarely, if ever, does just one thing at any time. For, The Great Multi-tasker does one thing that sets the stage for another thing and that other thing is the catalyst for a third thing and son on! He is the Great Facilitator! And nowhere in this book is that truth more apparent than when our Mandy Jo goes to church.

One Sunday evening while they were eating supper, Mrs. Pickrell asked, "Mandy Jo, how would you like to go to church tonight and thank our Lord, Jesus, for all the blessings that are in our lives? Also, I heard that the pastor's daughter, Anita and the choir will be singing a new arrangement of "Amazin' Grace" tonight."

Mandy Jo stopped eating and thought for a moment. She was like that. She only gave answers to important questions after she thought about them. Mandy Jo knew about Jesus from going to church before she got sick and also from the

Bible studies she had with her grandmother since then. "Yes, Gammy, that would be nice."

Mrs. Pickrell took special care when she combed Mandy Jo's hair. And when Mandy Jo got dressed up she looked so pretty! Mandy Jo got the Bible out of her top dresser drawer that her grandmother had given her for her tenth birthday present. She was so anxious to go that she didn't wait for her grandmother to tell her to go to the car. She ran outside and sat in the car as soon as she was dressed. Finally, Mrs. Pickrell hurried out of the house putting her gloves on. She got into the car, started it up and off to church they went.

It seemed to Mandy Jo that her grandmother was really driving slowly. Mandy Jo didn't know it but Mrs. Pickrell was waiting until the church service had already started so they could just quietly sit on the last pew and maybe not be noticed so much.

Mrs. Pickrell parked the car and they got out. They walked across the parking lot and up the sidewalk toward the large double doors. Mrs. Pickrell opened the door on the right and they stepped into the building. They walked across the foyer and Mrs. Pickrell pulled the inner door open and they walked into the sanctuary. The usher heard them. He turned and looked at Mandy Jo and looked at Mandy Jo *and looked at Mandy Jo*. Mrs. Pickrell looked right back at her. Then it seemed that everybody who sat in the back of the church was staring at Mandy Jo like she was the strangest sight they had ever seen. Mrs. Pickrell knew that they were not looking at the pretty white dress with the large sunflower print. Nor did they seem to see her silky, wavy black hair that hung so gracefully down her back. Her white patent leather shoes and her white matching purse were simply ignored. All they could see was Mandy Jo s grayish brown skin. Mrs. Pickrell knew that Mandy Jo probably looked very different to them but knew also that they could have been more sensitive and polite than they were.

Though the stares and pointing and the gasps and giggles were obvious, Mandy Jo didn't seem to notice. She just walked to the last pew with her back straight and her head held high and sat down. Mrs. Pickrell sat down next to her. Mandy Jo seemed more awed by the tall ceiling, the chandelier lights and stained glass windows than she was affected by the ill-mannered people who sat around her.

Mrs. Pickrell had loved little Mandy Jo from the first time she laid eyes on her in the hospital. But when she saw how brave and mature her granddaughter was at that moment, she loved her more than ever before and her heart sang with pride. She knew her granddaughter was very aware of the stares. Mandy Jo had an uncanny ability to sense when she was being the object of ridicule and spectacle. Mrs. Pickrell knew immediately that coming to church was a colossal mistake! But, the peace and self-control Mandy Jo was demonstrating confused her.

When they arrived, the organist and pianist were just starting to play the introduction to a song that Mrs. Pickrell didn't know would become Mandy Jo's favorite, "Amazing Grace." The choir was to hum the chords in accompaniment to the pastor's daughter, Anita, who would sing the words. Mandy Jo saw that some people were reading from their hymnals so she reached over to the bookrack on the pew in front of her. Picking up a hymnal, she said, "Gammy, will you find that song for me?" Mrs. Pickrell took the book and thumbed through the pages.

She heard the beautiful, low alto voice of Anita come in right on cue, "Amazin' Grace, how sweet the sound…." Her voice was mature and polished and Anita knew how to use it. Her college degree in voice was well earned. The congregation began to sway in time to the down home, heartfelt rendition.

By the time the choir got to the line that said, "…was blind but now I see," Mrs. Pickrell had found the right page. Mandy Jo was humming the tune with Anita and quickly learned the melody.

For some strange and wonderful reason, Mandy Jo stopped humming to herself and began to sing the words. She sang so softly, at first, that Mrs. Pickrell could barely hear her.

"Through many dangers, toils and snares," she whispered as if she was just thinking out loud. Then her little voice seemed to realize what she was saying. It was as if all of the pain and the sufferings that she had endured; all of the tears she knew she still must cry and all the joys she had ever anticipated of finally seeing Jesus face to face had come together in just this one moment. All of a sudden she began to sing louder in a slowly rising crescendo! Her sweet little soprano voice seemed to fill the back of the church and filter toward the front. The totally unexpected sound rose above the sound of Anita. The sound wasn't just louder – it was different. There was a life in it! There was Something so real in it! There was - *His Presence* in it! Those who sat near Mandy Jo were mesmerized by the silky, angelic voice. "…I have already come," she sang. "'Twas grace that brought me safe thus far.…"

Anita was moved by the sound of the youthful soprano voice. She was struck to the very core of her heart by the sound of the conviction of truth. The hauntingly beautiful, disembodied sound of a voice that knew more than just the melody and the words flooded Anita's heart. The new singer was evidently singing the pain of her emotions and the hope of her understandings; the misery of her realities and the exquisite ecstasy of her anticipation to be with her Lord. The words that Anita was singing seemed to just stick in her throat. All of a sudden, Anita's voice was a hollow sound in her own ears. For the first time in her life, Anita knew that she was witnessing someone sing of God's amazing grace just as she had always meant it in her own heart. She stopped singing and with everyone else, hunted through the church for the source of that voice. Anita discovered that the sound emanated from the tiny frame of a little girl. She couldn't help wondering how that young girl could know so much about life and God. It was apparent that the little singer was doing more than singing. She was expressing in a universal language, the hurts and pains and the delights and the elations; the confusions and the negative knowings of everyone there. This little wonder of wonders was mirroring and causing everyone there to see and relive scenes that were the most painful and the most exquisitely joyous experiences of their lives. These pivotal moments and experiences had ultimately done more than any one thing from their past, present or anticipated future to mold them into who and what they now were.

Most certainly, Anita's heart was laid bare. Anita tried to wrench her attention away from the pain that she thought she had put completely out of her mind. But there it was again! There was that old accusation and indictment against her Lord for her failed marriage. It was so hard to accept that God had allowed her friend, Sharee, who was known to be "easy" to get married and stay married while Anita remained alone and lonely for so long. Anita had waited to be intimate with a man until she was married. She had kept herself for her husband so that the Lord would be pleased and her husband would love and respect her. But Sharee was known to "sleep around."

Remembering the day that Ben had come home and told her that the company he worked for had gone out of business, Anita couldn't stop the tears from flowing. She had reassured Ben in every way that she knew that everything would be all right. But he couldn't and didn't find a job. She remembered the day that the finance company repossessed their car. Ben seemed to weather that storm but when the mortgage company foreclosed on their house and they were forced to move in with his parents, *Ben never recovered from that*! Now they argued all of the time about little things that were really not worth the trouble. And Ben had just last night said that he wanted a divorce so that Anita could find someone who could give her all the things he can't.

Anita had not wanted to accuse her God but whom else could she blame? Who else had the authority to decide who would be blessed and who would be cursed? Her confidence in her Lord was such that she knew that even *if He didn't choose* who would be happy and prosperous – *He at least had to consent* to it. Hence, her dilemma was, how could she continue to worship and to serve a God Who doesn't care about her feelings and her life?

When her father had requested that Anita sing the choir's newest addition to its repertoire, she had flinched at the thought because she didn't see where God's grace was all that amazing! She had even harbored the unsettling thought that if she was given the chance to be God for just one hour - *she could have done infinitely better than God had done!* She thought that she would never see anything "amazing" about God again!

But, there was Something promising in the way this child's words were filling Anita's heart. There was Something healing in the sound of her voice. Something alive that could give life was both heard and felt in this song of this singer. This child was singing with a quality of innocence and honesty that neither Anita nor any one of the members of the choir could produce. The elements of their character that put the price of this brand of innocence and honesty far out of their range were their own sophistication and their pride. Many were the times Anita had heard her father tell the congregation, "Your human feelings get you into trouble and your pride keeps you there!

Anita recognized that there was nothing in this little girl that was artificial; nothing about her was fake or pretentious. She was simple, natural, unaffected, and completely untainted by worldly wisdom. Further, she was totally at peace with herself and her God. She had no shadows in her heart that she kept hidden from the light of exposure. She was altogether transparent! She was purely unashamed of herself and her life. She was totally and blatantly - honest! She evidently knew that she had to apologize *for nothing.*

By the warm, soft aura of light that seemed to glow around this girl, all of the members of the congregation seemed to be able to see themselves. They all winced as what they saw reminded them of the faults and the failures that their pride would not allow them to expose to others. They knew that they were flawed and had been for a very long time. But they couldn't get help because they were too concerned about the possibility that their "helpers" might change their opinion of them. Indeed, their humanity had gotten them into trouble and *their pride <u>was</u> keeping them there*!

By the time that Mandy Jo got to the words, "…. and Grace will lead me home," the plaintive cry of her silvery voice had somehow replaced the sound of the choir. Each member of the choir was lost in a private reverie and sought to finally address their most painful realities. Most were very conflicted! They were engaged in various kinds of mental gymnastics. On the one hand, they wrestled in futile efforts to drive from their minds ghosts and shadows that would not be denied and on the other hand they tried to ignore their most painful memories.

Only the piano and the organ continued to be heard as the musicians played melody and counter-melody in masterful accompaniment to the angelic voice of little Mandy Jo.

Handkerchiefs and tissues seemed to materialize as everyone found their eyes welling up with tears. Emotional pains that many had been ignoring for years were healed as Mandy Jo sang that evening. Answers for many unanswered questions were rendered unnecessary and the spirit to forgive cascaded over souls that had borne grudges and resentments too long to remember the "Why" of their feuds.

Mrs. Pickrell doubted that Mandy Jo even realized when she stood up. She watched and was awed with the rest of the congregation when, with lilting voice, Mandy Jo declared:

> *"Twas Grace that taught my heart to fear*
> *And Grace my fears relieved.*
> *How precious did that Grace appear*
> *The hour I first believed."*

No one really knew the extent of the spiritual sickness and weariness that had pervaded the church. For a very long time the congregation had been in dire need of revival and renewal. A measure of the degree of the problem was the fact that nobody in the church seemed to realize that they'd had no new converts nor seen any miracles in a long time.

The pastor had been contemplating giving up the church for something that was less burdensome and more exciting - *until Mandy Jo sang!* Most members of the church had not realized it but they were only coming to the church because it was, after all, their church – *until Mandy Jo sang!* Others were simply coming out of a habit long ago acquired. Some of the deacons had not been on speaking terms with one another – *before Mandy Jo sang!* Choir members were delivered of long held jealousies and backsliders recommitted their lives to Christ *while Mandy Jo sang,*

> *"When we've been there ten thousand years,*
> *Bright, shining as the sun.*
> *We've no less days to sing God's praise*
> *Than when we first begun."*

For the first time in years, the hope that the words of the song spelled out became real to the church. The hymn that had been sung for the past fifty years in the church was finally heard. The second coming of the Lord, Jesus, was envisioned with clarity and was indelibly printed on every heart in a way that the body of believers had never experienced. The woes of yesterday and the trials of today were eclipsed by the joyous anticipation and celebration of tomorrow's victory *because Mandy Jo sang!*

Mandy Jo could do more than imagine the effects of the woes of the church! She could sense them and feel them! She had a built in "pain detector" that enabled her to diagnose and absorb the feelings that others around her were experiencing! She then cared enough to incorporate into her singing the awareness of their hurt and the love, joy and peace that was their balm and their healing!

CHAPTER 9

WITH GREAT CARING COMES GREAT RESPONSIBILITY

Sometimes it seems to be a tossup as to who is most influenced by the process of Watching! Is it the Watcher or the one Watched?

It was Mrs. Pickrell's laundry day. This was the day she did all of the washing and ironing for the week. Mandy Jo's grandmother had just put another load of clothes in the washing machine and was taking the ironing board into the kitchen to begin ironing the load of clothes she had taken off the clothes line.

Mandy Jo had awakened early and was lying on her bed looking out of the window. She was careful not to let the morning sun touch her skin. The thoughts that flooded her mind were of her time in church last Sunday. Mandy Jo had decided last night that she would open up and tell her Grandmother how she felt about her experience at church last Sunday. She was sure that her grandmother really didn't know what she had gone through and how she had been affected by it all. Mandy Jo rolled off the bed and landed on her feet.

She got her bathrobe that was lying at the foot of her bed, put it on and walked into the living room looking for her grandmother. Then she heard the creak of the old ironing board as if it was groaning in protest of the pressure that was being put on it.

"Gammy?" Mandy Jo called softly.

"Why, good morning, Mandy Jo." Mrs. Pickrell looked up from the baby blue blouse with the puffy sleeves that was Mandy Jo's favorite and noticed that her granddaughter seemed to have something on her mind this morning. "What is it, baby?" Mandy Jo's only family in the world gently answered.

Mandy Jo walked over to one of the hardback wooden chairs at the kitchen table. She forgot to pick the chair up like her Grandmother always told her to. She scraped the floor with the chair and looked down to see if she had torn the linoleum. With a quick sigh of relief, she saw that no damage had been done.

Mandy Jo sat down in the chair and looked up at her Grandmother. "I don't want to go back to church again!" she blurted out.

That totally surprised Mrs. Pickrell who had no idea that it bothered her at all! "Why didn't you say something Sunday, Mandy Jo?"

"Gammy, you always told me that the best way to deal with someone's bad manners is with my good manners. So I just ignored those people then. I really didn't go to churc00h to see *them*. I just had to see them 'cause they were there."

Then Mandy Jo put a look on her face that suggested that she was many years older than her twelve. "Besides, I know how my sickness makes me feel and it wasn't hard to know how those people who all have a different sickness may be hurting. What really made me understand and care is when we were walking up the sidewalk to the church, my skin cancer started acting up and because I was hurting I didn't want anybody else to be in pain. But I could tell that some of them had been hurting for a long time. And I could see that many of their wounds were deep. Couldn't you tell how scared some of those people were, Gammy?"

Mrs. Pickrell looked at Mandy Jo quizzically for what must have been a long minute. Many were the questions that passed through her mind as she considered that her granddaughter was truly wise beyond her years.

"Mandy Jo, how could you tell that those people were hurting and scared? Even I didn't see all of that. Now that you've mentioned, it, though, I know you're right. I mean, I know some of what many of them are going through with sons in jail and daughters having unwanted pregnancies and some have terrible physical sicknesses. Then there are those whose loved ones are away fighting in the war. These are tormented everyday with fears that their husbands or sons, fathers or mothers, sisters or brothers will die. But I am amazed that *you* could sense their pain and fears", Gammy concluded.

Mandy Jo looked down at her hands and said, "I don't know how it is that I can see so much *that I am sure nobody wants me to see*! But, I do understand things and I care about them." Her voice sounded so small to the wise grandmother who loved her so much. Then Many Jo asked, "Gammy, why do I feel so…so…." She was searching for just the right word. "Why do I feel so *responsible* for the people whose pain I can see? I want to do something *for them* or *to them* or even *with them* to make their hurt go away. I know *my* hurt will only go away when I die. So I want to make their hurt go away while I live!"

"Baby, you would not be the Mandy Jo that I know and love if you didn't care. You have always cared about people who are in pain. It's as if the good Lord has filled your heart up with His love and has decided to love everybody in your life through you. Everyone doesn't or maybe can't care like you care. But one thing I know is that everybody you love knows that they have been loved with a very special affection and in a very unique and wonderful way!

The wistful Grandmother stopped talking for a moment. Then with a faraway look in her eyes continued, "You know, Mandy Jo, my daughter, your mother was like that. As a matter of fact, I have wondered if Jesus took her at such a young age because of the great weight and burden that was always on her shoulders. Your mother gave herself to every pain and distress that came into the life of those around her."

"Your mother's feelings, heart and strength never belonged to herself alone. She lived for everybody else. The only time she gave herself to herself was when she let everything go so she could give you love and attention. And in those, what I call, "Mother Moments," your mother came alive in ways that nothing else could inspire."

Mandy Jo was caught between two thoughts that pulled at her from opposite directions. It sounded like her grandmother was talking to herself and saying things that may have been for her grandmother to know alone. But there were so many things about her mother that she had forgotten and perhaps more that she had never known. She didn't think she should stay where her grandmother was if her grandmother was thinking her private thoughts out loud. But Mandy Jo just couldn't bring herself to go out of the room! She did not merely *want to hear about her mother. She needed to hear everything that she could about her mother!*

"She loved you with a love that could have been measured in tons, miles and celestial heights," her Gammy continued. "She gave all the love she could to heal those who were hurting from loneliness, from physical pain and from fears too horrendous to describe. But she reserved the best of her love for you, Baby Girl. Mandy Jo, your mother could afford to give this kind of love to you because you were pure, innocent and fresh. The negative effects of life had not touched your soul. She knew that it was only a matter of time, though, before the love that sheltered you would find that its caring arms were too short to protect you from many of life's harsh realities. And she was determined that you would know from her that you have been loved wholly, purely, unselfishly and that somehow after you had grown up you would define that love in one word – *satisfying*."

Her voice low and soft, Mrs. Pickrell slowed her speech as her thoughts ran their course. The silence was almost tangible when she finished speaking. The mood in the kitchen was pensive but calm.

Mandy Jo's pet canary was in her cage in the living room. In the solitude and quiet of the moment the canary began to sing. The bird's song was harmonious with the mood that saturated the kitchen. It served to remind Mrs. Pickrell of the song that was the ministry of the Sunday morning worship service.

"Mandy Jo, Mrs. Pickrell said, changing the subject, "I never knew you could sing so beautifully *and with such feeling!*"

"Well, Gammy, when I first started singing, I was just enjoying the pretty song. But as I read the words in the songbook, I began to think of all of the things that I've been through. I couldn't help remembering that my mommy and daddy are dead. Somehow, all the nights that I lay in my bed, hugging my pillow and wishing it was my Mommy became so real that I missed her like I've never missed her before! Then, I remembered that I will never know how my daddy's arms feel as he holds me and makes me to know that nothing will ever hurt me."

Mandy Jo reached up and began to caress the ebony locks of her long wavy hair. She said, "I thank you, Gammy, for all the things you do for me but while I was singing that song, I wondered how it would be for my mother to comb and brush my hair. I wondered how her perfume smells and how she really sounds because now it is getting so hard to remember her voice. I remembered how my daddy's beard used to scratch my face when he kissed me in the morning. It used to tickle me and we used to laugh so hard together! Oh, Gammy, I felt so much that day; so much joy and so much sadness!"

The tears began to seep past Mrs. Pickrell's eyelids and down her gentle face as Mandy Jo continued, "I couldn't help thinking the questions that I have never had answers to. The questions are, "Why did my mommy and daddy have to die?'" and *"Why did I have to go and get skin cancer?"*

It cut Mrs. Pickrell to the core of her heart when Mandy Jo whispered her concerns in her brave little voice. Now, Mandy Jo was talking to her grandmother and looking toward the open window but was seeing way beyond the backyard, the alley and anything in her neighborhood. The sound of her voice was like the breath of an angel softly caressing the room, "I know how much you love me, Gammy, but I got so sad that day. For the first time, I realized that when I die - *you will be all alone!* I know my skin cancer is not my fault but sometimes I feel like it will be so mean of me to die and leave you all alone."

Mandy Jo seemed to realize that she had stepped out for a minute and brought herself back to the kitchen and said, "As I sang 'Amazing Grace,' it seemed that I felt all of the sadness I had ever known fill up my heart and I just tried to sing it all out."

Mrs. Pickrell finally realized that she was wiping tears away from her eyes. She had long since stopped ironing. As though there was something on her hands, Mrs. Pickrell wiped he hands on her apron and said, "Come here, Mandy Jo," with her arms outstretched.

Mandy Jo seemed to be waiting for just this moment for she ran over to her "Gammy" and fell into her arms! Mandy Jo's eyes were brimming over with tears. Wise beyond her years she was but at this time, in this place enfolded into her grandmother's bosom, she just felt like a twelve years old little girl who needed to be loved, held and reassured.

"Mandy Jo, Jesus is not just my Lord and my God - *He is my best friend!* I don't want you to ever worry about me because my Best Friend will never leave me alone! I have had Jesus in my life ever since I was a teenager. It was He Who kept me all these years when it looked like my world was being uprooted from its foundation and I couldn't go on. It was the very real friendship of the Greatest Love of All that buoyed me up when the cruel waters of life flooded over my soul with more force and burden than I ever thought I could endure."

The old woman took her granddaughter by both arms and stood her straight up in front of her, "Girl, *your Gammy is in the best of Hands!* I won't say that I won't miss you because I love you more than I love my own life! But you've got to know that Jesus is more comfort *for me* than you being here is *to me*! I don't think you can understand that yet. But trust me! *I will never be alone!*"

They never saw Mandy Jo in church again after that because she never went back. She never knew or imagined the great extent that God used her to make so many positive changes in the church that day. Of course, she never saw herself as anybody special anyway! To her, she was just Mandy Jo. Not Mandy. Not Jo, just Mandy Jo. But to the church, she would always be, *"The Wounded Healer!"*

As for Mrs. Pickrell, she never had to wonder "Why?" again about Mandy Jo's illness nor her daughter's and her husband's untimely deaths.

For a long time after that service, many said that God used Mandy Jo to save the church because many people were planning to leave the church *before Mandy Jo sang!* The pastor told everyone that an angel had visited the church that day. It was the pastor who first called Mandy Jo a "Wounded Healer".

In this story we find that while Mrs. Pickrell was the "Watcher" for Mandy Jo, Mandy Jo was the "Watcher" for the congregation at the church. This is the way that the Great Multi-tasker works.

Please do not miss the contrast between the peace that secured the heart of Mrs. Pickrell and the lack of the same that tortured Mandy Jo! Mrs. Pickrell rested in God to the point where she either never harbored the unsettling questions that stymied Many Jo or she had such an abiding trust in her God that the answers were totally unnecessary!

It isn't only her youth that is the reason for Mandy Jo having so many unanswerable questions about the events of her life! It is most assuredly the lack of intimacy with God that in and of itself provides the peace and sense of security that Mandy Jo so needed! There is an intimacy with God that can make answers to unanswerable questions COMPLETELY UNECESSARY!

CHAPTER 10

TRUST THE MASTER WATCHER

Picture it! Standing in the boat, Jesus has just taught a multitude of people who were seated and standing on the shore. From His place on the boat His voice carried to them new life; new hope. He had already promised the people a new order; the possibility of a new and personal relationship with God.

Finally, fatigued and worn, Jesus sends the multitude away. And the man, Christ Jesus, succumbs to the frailty of human flesh and lays his head down to rest.

Picture it! Jesus is asleep in a boat on the Sea of Galilee where a silent specter has a diabolical agenda. Satan remembered the promise Jehovah made to him in the beginning when First Man and First Woman failed in Eden. "He shall bruise your head but _you shall bruise His heel._" Supposing that this was his opportunity, the Great Deceiver seizes the moment. He knows that all who go out on the waters where the Prince of the Power of the Air has won many a victory over man have always been at his mercy. Satan speaks to the winds and commands the waves. He almost salivates with fiendish delight in anticipation of the death of his nemesis, Jesus, the Son of God. A storm quickly rises for Satan realizes that he has Jesus right where he wants Him. The devil commands his demons and they stir up the air until the wind causes the waves to toss the boat like a match box on the water. Satan remembers the Words of Jehovah. "Ye shall bruise His heel!" The enemy of God is so anxious that he can't wait. He decides that this will be the day when the Son of God will lay in defeat at the feet of His arch enemy. He doesn't realize that Jesus was destined to die by the shedding of His Blood. "For without the shedding of blood is no remission." (Hebrew (:22) The winds and the waves are so violent that the disciples fear the boat will capsize. They hold out no hope that they will survive this storm.

Isn't this so like man? Why do we always possess a greater knowledge of our negative circumstance than we do the positive Love, Power and Integrity that characterizes our Lord? Jesus was no less the Son of God because He was asleep. Remember, Jesus was the God-man! There was a part of Him that did tire and require sleep but there was another part of Him that "neither sleeps nor slumbers"; a part that remains ever vigilant! It is so remarkable that despite all the miracles that many believers have experienced at the hands of our faithful God they still have a tendency to believe in the earthly and temporal more than the Heavenly and Eternal.

Forgotten was the fact that the God of the water, wind, rain and waves was on board the ship. Their problem was that they were in the boat at the same time that Jesus was but – they *were not_with Him_ in the boat!* Had they been with Jesus in the boat they would have not panicked! To be there at the same time as He was only suggests that they were in close physical proximity to Him. However, to be with Him in the boat is to be totally and completely aware of His Identity, His Power, His agenda and His great love for you.

It must be pointed out that Jesus and company were not on a battleship. They were on a small fishing vessel on a storm tossed sea! How is it that Jesus lie asleep in the boat yet remained separate from and unaffected by the violence of the storm tossed sea? How is it that the unpredictably twisting, wind driven boat left Jesus undisturbed and resting? The answer is as profound as it is comforting. Being the Prince of Peace, <u>nothing</u> could disturb His tranquility when He decided to be at rest. Jesus does not merely have peace *He is Peace!* He doesn't only feel peaceful - He is Peace in a Body!

The disciples woke Jesus with one of the greatest insults to His character that He had ever received. "Carest Thou not that we perish?" they argued. Jesus simply got up and spoke to the winds and the waves, "Peace be still!" The storm immediately abated. Calm was restored.

You know, this writer would rather Jesus be on board asleep than have everyone in the world on board wide awake! Jesus knew that though His flesh needed rest the Father and the Holy Spirit aspect of His Entity did not! Though the devil thought he had Jesus at his mercy - Jesus was really never in any danger! So were the disciples safe in the security of the Prince of Peace!

What an awesome and profound idea! What peace this affords the believer! God is completely aware of and supremely able to control, restrict and order every issue that comes into our life. In the final analysis, the child of the King has nothing to worry about for GOD IS and is in total charge of His children and their destiny! The learned Psalmist, King David, said, "My times are in His hands."

It is no great wonder that the Word of God could of a truth declare, "No weapon that is formed against thee shall prosper; and every tongue that shall rise against thee in judgment thou shalt condemn. This is the heritage of the servants of the LORD, and their righteousness is of me, saith the LORD." (Isaiah 54:17). He not only could see down the line of time to when our enemy would desire to fight against us - God was there in the devil's war room and knows what the enemy planned! God is an unseen spectator at the meeting when our enemies decide why they would target God's own. And He witnesses them form their devilish reasons that they would wage war against God's forgiven ones.

Why don't we just trust the Lord? The bard wrote:

> *"Oh what peace we often forfeit,*
> *Oh what needless pains we bare.*
> *All because we do not carry*
> *Everything to God in prayer".*

For man to be truly dependent on God but refuse to depend on Him is so without good reason. Jesus taught, *"Without me ye can do nothing." (John 15:5)*

CHAPTER 11

"WHEN THE MASTER WATCHER WATCHES"

What do you do when you cannot live with losing but there seems to be no way that you can win? What do you do when the stakes are so high that not overcoming is not a viable option? Add to the equation the reality that to all intents and purposes all is really lost and there is not even the hint of possibility that you can win! All whose reasons are founded in rational judgment are of the same consensus - YOU HAVE ALREADY LOST THE BATTLE!

Amid the din of the noisy crowd the old champion sat on his stool in the red corner. He didn't seem to hear them but the arena was filled with fans who loved the old veteran. Many cried *out for him to throw in the towel before some permanent damage was done. Other die hard believers in the heavy weight champion of the world, Chester Strong, shouted words of encouragement to the bludgeoned fighter.

The mouse under his right eye and the cut over his left eye were only the beginning of his troubles. The champ had thrown everything he had at the young challenger. And though the young fighter was visibly shaken more than a few times, he just wouldn't go down. Chester Strong was knocked down twice in the previous round and only the bell saved me from going down the third time.

He tried to focus his attention on what his trainer was saying. But all he could seem to see was the man in the long white hospital coat with a stethoscope around his neck.

"If she doesn't have the kidney transplant by Friday, Bianca will die!" the doctor announced to Chester and Mrs. Strong. Chester knew that he didn't have close to the fifty-seven thousand dollars that the operation cost. But he knew that even the losing purse for the fight was much more than enough for the operation. If only he hadn't allowed his big mouthed opponent to goad him into agreeing that the winner would get all the money - the winning prize as well as the loser's prize money.

Chester heard the bell that ordered him back into the ring. With every ounce of strength at his disposal he willed himself back into the ring where his young opponent was already dancing and bobbing. Chester felt so alone! There was no one who could help him now. He wondered how many of the fans really cared if he won or lost. He wondered how many just wanted to see a knock out and did not care who went down. He further wondered how many would simply jump to the side of the new champ and how many would never forget the old warrior.

At that moment neither the millions of fans that watched the fight on pay-per-view nor the twenty thousand screaming boxing fans that lusted for blood were a part of the world of

Chester Strong. His purpose for living was not to entertain this maddened throng. It dawned on Chester that his entire world (for the next few minutes) was the twenty by twenty boxing ring and one room in the state's largest hospital - the room where his little Bianca hovered between life and death. The entire population of his world was four: his Bianca, himself, his challenger and the referee. His purpose was not just to shut the challenger's disrespectful mouth; it was not just to win the championship! It was to win the prize money so that his little Bianca could live!

The pummeling fists of the challenger seemed to be locked on the chin, jaw and stomach of Chester. The blows were coming so fast that Chester didn't know whether to block them or try to connect with one to his own. When he tried to counter punch he left himself open and felt the most painful jabs of his career. And when he tried to use his forearms to protect himself, the blows rained on him with such fury that he reeled backward across the ring!

Chester had long given up the hope that his opponent would punch himself out. This young challenger actually seemed to be stronger this round than the last. What was Chester going to do? What could he do?

He tried to focus on the battle but the thought kept screaming in his mind, "If you lose this fight -YOU WILL HAVE KILLED BIANCA!"

For the first time in his life Chester began to experience a feeling that he had only heard about. It was more than fear of losing. It was the certainty that he could not win!

As the rights and lefts connected he remembered the referee saying between rounds, "If you don't fight back, Champ, I'm going to stop this fight!" Right now, Chester wanted to say to the referee, "If you think you can do better you're welcome to try."

He shook his head to try to bring some clarity to his vision. But all he could see was his little Bianca lying in that little hospital bed that made tiny Bianca seem too small to be real.

Somehow (thinking that he was hallucinating from the constant battering of rock hard fists) he saw himself in Bianca's room. He knew that the scene depicted his visit last night just before he left to go home. She was asleep as he knelt beside her bed. She was so still! He saw himself check to see if her chest was moving. Not being a religious man, Chester was surprised to hear himself praying to God. The champ had never even been sure that God exists. Now he was praying to him. "God, I am not sure that you are there. And if You are there I don't know if You will hear me pray. I know I have never taken time to talk to You before but please believe me I hope You are there! Bianca needs You and maybe I need You too. If You will work this out so that my baby will be all right, I will know that You are real and that You love me and my family. And I promise You that I will love You and serve You for the rest of my life".

Chester was now fighting partly because he knew the consequences of losing and partly by instinct. He was not only a fighter - he was a champion and he knew *that he was fighting for a life that was more important to him than was his own.*

He knew that he was too weak to do any damage - BUT HE HAD TO TRY ONE MORE TIME! Out of sheer desperation, left-handed Chester marshaled all the strength that he had. He put his whole body into the swing and threw his Sunday punch - a roundhouse left hook to the jaw.

Then he saw it! The looping right cross! But it was coming so fast that he couldn't get out of the way! It connected with his left cheek at the same time that the champ felt his glove connect. A brilliant flash of light was all the veteran saw. The brilliant radiance suddenly gave way to a thick enveloping darkness.

Chester, thinking he must have lain there for hours, woke to the sound of a crowd gone mad in their cheering frenzy. Even before his eyes opened he heard the referee counting, "…five, six." An instinct born of years of training took over and he knew that he had to get up fast! Struggling and falling back, he heard the referee say, "Seven". The champ jerked himself up with a great groan and by the time he heard the referee yell, "…eight," he was on his feet. The great champion was still too dazed to realize what had happened when he felt his right hand being lifted in the universal sign of victory.

It was back in the dressing room that Chester found out how he won the fight. Everybody congratulated him on throwing the hardest punch of the fight. They talked about it being perfectly timed and artfully thrown. Chester knew that he could barely remember throwing that blow. All he really knew was that he was so glad that the hardest fight in his career was over!

It slowly dawned on him. He had won! Bianca won't die! *His baby will live!* He thought that his heart would burst with joy. His precious Bianca will be all right!

As the champ thought about these things, the realization that he had won gave birth to the understanding that the impossible had happened. His mind screamed the obvious question, "HOW?"

Suddenly, with startling clarity, Chester Strong knew how the victory was his. God had proven to him that He is real and that the Lord truly loved him and his Bianca.

With a grateful heart he knelt on the floor oblivious to his trainers, the cut man, and the cadre of reporters with the rest of his entourage. Through broken and cut lips he prayed, "Thank You, my Lord, Jesus. For the first time in my life I know that You are real. I can think of a hundred reasons that you would have for loving my Bianca. But for the life of me, I don't understand why You love me! But I know as surely as I know my name that You do love me! Thank You for this new opportunity to start a new life with you! Thank you for this miracle! My daughter was as good as dead. But by Your Grace and Mercy she will live. And not only will she live but I will live in You and for You. If You will lead me, I promise You, I will find out everything I need to know about how to live for You. *And I will live for You for the rest of my Life!" The Master Watcher sees more than the physical situation. He sees the desires and intents of the heart If man could ever learn the measure of the Love of God toward humanity, every life could be lived in such great peace and comfort. Because of His Love and Compassion, God is totally unable to see us fail when we come to me for the strength to win!*

"When I am weak then am I strong" were the words of the Apostle, Paul. He further expresses the divine promise, "My

strength is made perfect in weakness". One astute observer of life has recorded, "Man's extremity is God's opportunity". Let us settle this in our hearts forever! Whatever we need Me to do - GOD CAN DO IT! Jesus is The Great Enabler!

CHAPTER 12

"WATCH WHO YOU WATCH FOR!"

It is in the nature of every Watcher to watch. However, it is incumbent upon each Watcher to know for whom he is watching and the purpose of the vigil so as to not strengthen and protect the hands of the wicked.

"Watch out for old Peep for me," ordered Junebug as he looked back over his shoulder. Junebug was the ten-year-old brother of Peewee who was only seven years old. Junebug pulled up his drooping blue jeans that were more patches than pants.

He had to stand on his toes to reach the top shelf of the candy counter. Junebug's eyes were bright and alive with anticipation. He could hardly wait to fill his mouth with the taste of his favorite candy - "Good and Plenty." The pink and black candy seemed too whisper promises of sugary delight as they nestled between the "'Mary Janes" and the "Squirrel Nuts".

"Look around the corner of the aisle and see what old Peep is doing, Peewee." The kids called Mr. Peoples "old

Peep" because he always seemed to be peeping over his round wire rimmed glasses. He wore them just at the tip of his pointed nose. One of the reasons the guys didn't really like him was because he wouldn't let them read the new comic books without paying for them.

"Look around the corner of the aisle and see what old Peep is doing," Junebug ordered.

Peewee walked over to the end of the aisle. The sole of his right shoe flapping with every step he took. One of his suspenders seemed to always hang behind him causing one of his pants legs to be lower than the other. He peeked around the corner past the display of "wind mill cookies and saw Mr. Peoples waiting on a customer. Mr. Peoples was handing an elderly lady of small band of groceries.

"I'm scared!" Peewee whispered, as he tried to blink back one little tear that sneaked through his eyelid and trickle down his left cheek. "This is wrong! What if you get caught?"

Junebug laughed, "What are you worrying about? You're not doing anything wrong! If you're too chicken to get some candy for yourself at least you can watch Old Peep for me!"

Junebug got a box of Good and Plentys from the shelf. He opened them and Peewee could smell the candy all the way over to where he was. Junebug had a way of making everything he ate look, smell and sound sooo gooood! He didn't just take a few pieces of candy out of a box. He turned the box up to his mouth and filled his mouth with good and Plentys. He chewed and smacked and smacked and smacked and chewed!

It looked sooo gooood! But peewee knew that stealing was wrong! He knew that Jesus is always watching his children and when his children are obedient and honest, Jesus is so proud of them. So, Peewee didn't want to steal. He didn't even want to the lookout for Junebug. But he knew that Junebug would laugh at him and tell all the guys that he was chicken. And besides, Peewee liked Junebug and really wanted to be his friend. Peewee always chewed on his shirt collar when he was scared and nervous and now he was chewing his collar all the way down to the first button.

"What would Mom and Pad think of me if they knew what I am doing? I really like Mr. Peoples. Anyway, he would probably give us some candy if I asked for it. I don't have to steal from me and I won't!" little Peewee thought.

Peewee's mind was made up to tell Junebug that he was not going to help him steal by looking out for Mr. Peoples. But all of a sudden Peewee heard footsteps! Someone was coming! Peewee looked between the shelves and caught a glimpse of Mr. Peoples coming toward the back of the store. He panicked! Gone were the thoughts of not helping Junebug. All he could think of was, "We are going to get caught it!"

"Here comes old Peep!" Peewee warned. Junebug heard the footsteps and realized that he wouldn't have time to hide the half empty candy box before he was caught. He thought fast! "Here, Peewee!" Junebug said, as he pushed the box into Peewee's hands - just before Mr. Peoples came around the corner!!

It is not unusual for the innocent to be taken advantage of by the cunning. Actually, this injustice had its origin in the garden called "Eden" when First Woman found herself to be no match for the nefarious and totally treacherous mind of the serpent. Jesus' admonishment to be "wise as serpents and harmless as doves" (Matt. 10:16) is not to be taken lightly!

However, one must be ever vigilant because our adversary the devil, as a roaring lion, walketh about seeking whom he may devour" (Ist Pet 5:8)

CHAPTER 13

"I DON'T HAVE A WATCHER AND I DON'T TRUST YOURS!"

In the book of Ephesians, chapter two and verse twelve, the Apostle, Paul, reminds the Christian of the time when all men were in a spiritual state that the Apostle describes as "…having no hope and without God in the world". What a terrible place to find oneself without hope – <u>this world!</u> What a terrible and miserable place to be devoid of the Living Presence of a Living God! Perhaps few can say without fear of contradiction what may be found <u>on other worlds!</u> But we can all attest to what is evidenced on this planet. <u>And the evidence proves we need hope in God more than anything else in this world</u>. There are many things in this life that one can live without and still enjoy true success in relative safety - <u>but hope and God are not numbered among them!</u>

There is more in this life that is antagonistic to one surviving and prospering than the number of things that are supportive to one's success. Hence, there is the need for a "Watcher". When one has "no hope" and is "without God in this world" – <u>one is</u>

definitely at risk! For, it is one's hope and the Almighty Power and Grace of God that is one's mainstay. To lack this divine dynamic duo is to invite certain and absolute destruction. If the hopeless and Godless are to survive in this world, there is a grave need for a Watcher! Someone must hope and trust in God that the hopeless will find hope and that the godless will be found by God. If the hopeless and Godless won't seek God – some Watcher must! For, the driving influences of the true Watcher are his hope and his God.

It was eight o'clock in the autumn evening. The sun was changing from the brilliant, blinding yellow orb that had spilled its golden rays and buttered the skyscape. Colors blended with colors in the sky. The kaleidoscope of coloration moved in slow motion to evolve from a yellow tinted baby blue to a rose hue and was now becoming a mauve wonder of Divine inspiration. When the Master Muralist gave His cue, the genial nightshade began slowly and gently lowering to reveal the first hint of the diamond-like sparkles of stars that would light the world this night. The silvery pale light of the moon had not yet begun to bathe the soon to be deep dark blue of the night in its soft twilight. Glistening stars were only just beginning their flirtatious winking at all that is the world of the night.

Kitty Satterwhite was sixteen years old. Her oval face and quick, almond shaped, hazel eyes were often opened wide in joy and surprise as she gave vent to her love of life. The corners of her mouth seemed always to promise a smile. The gentle mahogany of her skin was complimented by the soft wavy hair that framed her face as it hung down in a page boy hairstyle.

The calm that blanketed this dusky time of the early evening belied the fact that a war was being waged in Europe. There was nothing in the air that even hinted that German bombers were at that moment delivering their very lethal cargo to the city that was London in England.

Children who were not ready to surrender the day were still playing tag in the street. Those who were reluctant to go indoors were slowly appreciating the street lamps. From the sidewalk, the glow of pipes and cigars shone intermittently on the porches where elderly men were sitting. The flickering lights gave the impression of fireflies courting and signaling to one another in the autumn night. The aromatic flavor of the smoke was a warm and familiar experience on the block. Murmurings of indistinct voices in quiet conversation carried from porch to porch. This was the sound of home and family; of neighborhood and safety. It was the sound of freedom and right. It was the familiar and comforting world of Kitty Satterwhite.

Kitty was so full of life and so sensitive to those around her. She laughed quickly and loved much. In her passion for life, she could find herself angry, discontented or confused as the situation warranted. At the awkward and confusing age known as adolescence, she knew she was not a little girl anymore but knew that she was not an adult either. She didn't know where she belonged and thought that probably her grandmother didn't know either. The problem was - she felt that her grandmother still treated her as she did when Kitty was twelve years old.

She wasn't "boy crazy" as her grandmother believed. She was just seeing them differently than she ever had before.

Some people called her a tomboy but Kitty was just proud that she could outrun, out jump and out throw almost every boy in her school. She was even one of the first players to be picked for a team when a baseball or basketball game was to be played.

Things were happening and changing in Kitty's life with alarming swiftness. Not only was Kitty rethinking and redefining her world and her place in it, she was also dealing with the new and confusing way that others saw her. Take for instance the time that her lifelong playmate, Butch Rafferty, had been so mesmerized by something *he newly saw* in Kitty that he didn't hear Mr. Turner called on him to go to the blackboard in their Algebra class. The class had snickered when Mr. Turner called on Butch twice.

"Mr. Rafferty!" He always called the students, "Mr." or "Miss."

"Mr. Rafferty, come to the blackboard and work this next problem!" Mr. Turner called. But Butch didn't hear a thing. Sitting across the aisle from Kitty, he was just staring at her with a look on his face that told everyone that he had mentally stepped out for a moment. His hands were clasped under his chin and his head was tilted at an angle. The way his eyes were glazed over caused everyone in the room to wonder if he was seeing Kitty across the aisle from me or gazing at a vision of loveliness far away in the recesses of his mind.

Mr. Turner put a finger to his lips, motioning for the class to remain quiet. He walked over to Butch and softly spoke in his ear, "Isn't she gorgeous?" Butch must have thought that the question was coming from his own mind.

"Yeah man! Oh yeah. Ain't that the truth!" Butch said with a dreamy sigh. The class howled. The guys high fived one another and mimicked Butch in a high pitched, falsetto voice, "Yeah man! Oooh, yeeaah, ain't *that* the truth!" Butch's face turned as red as his dark brown complexion could turn. But Butch had then done something she never imagined he would do - he'd looked straight at Kitty and given her the biggest boldest grin she had ever seen on his face.

Kitty had been so embarrassed that she covered her face with her hands and put her head down on her desk. She had been totally mortified but at the same time she had been surprised at the feeling of pleasure and wonder that filled her heart.

She had been reluctant to face the girls after class but got the second surprise of the day when they all came to her squealing and laughing in the hall after class. They were all so proud and envious of her because of the way Butch had been so captivated by her.

In her bedroom, she now examined, for the umpteenth time, the U.S. stamp that was the greatest treasure in her stamp collection. The young fifteen-year-old girl wondered if she would ever go to the United States of America. Kitty Satterwhite was reaching for the soft cloth she used to wipe the face of her stamp collection. Suddenly, the serenity of the moment was shattered by the piercing, screaming wail of the siren that declared danger. But she could not yet hear the ominous drone of the bomber planes that attacked so swiftly and with such deadly force.

Kitty had a fleeting thought. She wondered why she was putting the stamps into the top drawer of her dresser. She knew that it really wouldn't matter if she left them out or put them away if a bomb hit the house. But, somehow, she had the feeling that if she left everything in its place, the order that she left would insure that all will be in order upon her return. Snatching the closet door open, she grabbed her coat and scarf and ran into the living room where her grandmother sat in her rocking chair knitting a sweater.

"Grandmother," Kitty exclaimed. "Don't you hear the siren?" Why are you sitting there? We've got to go to the bomb shelter! *It's* our *only hope for survival!"*

Knitting needles clicking at a slow but steady pace came to a stop as the grandmother looked up at the fifteen-year-old girl. For what seemed to the young girl to be a long minute, the old woman just stared thoughtfully at her young charge.

"You go on, baby, Grandmother will be all right," she finally responded.

You mean you are not going to the bomb shelter?"

"No. Not this time. But I'll be all right, Kitty. You run on now and get to the shelter before they close the doors."

Chapter 14

I DON'T WANT TO LEAVE YOU
BUT I CAN'T DIE WITH YOU

It is so important that God's people develop an intimacy with God that inures to a relationship that has trust as its foundation!

Now it was the teenager's turn to grow thoughtful. Kitty gazed down at her grandmother and saw the familiar, but saw also some things she had never noticed before. She saw her grandmother's hair combed back into the same bun that she had worn for years. But Kitty slowly realized that sometime during the recent year's grandmother's hair had turned a gentle silver. The hands that were always so deft and sure, so strong and steady were even now shaking with a perceptible tremor. The skin on her face and hands had folds and wrinkles that seemed to complete the ensemble of age, wisdom and labors done. She wondered when this had all happened. She never even saw it coming. Kitty saw that her grandmother, whose carriage had always been regal and so majestic, was now unsure and tentative. The once so straight shoulders were now rounded and bowed with age.

When had all this age taken place? When had her lively and quick grandmother become an *old grandmother?* And how long had she been so tired looking; so worn and frail? Even her voice that in days gone by was so strong and vibrant now sounded weak and strained.

The only things about her grandmother that seemed to defy time and toil were her eyes. Those knowing, compassionate eyes. They seemed to see deep into one's soul while inviting one into the warmth and comfort of their understanding. They were eyes that refused to allow time and life to diminish their vitality and darkened their light. Those eyes promised to see far beyond the veneer of physical reality. They agreed to see truth no matter the cost. Those eyes held at the ready - the hope and the pledge that they are ever prepared to see something better if shown.

Kitty leaned down and put her arms around her grandmother and declared, "I can't just leave you Grandmother. If anything happens to you, *I'll have nobody!* So, let me get your coat and *let's just go while we still have time!*"

The wise grandmother had done her best to teach Kitty that God is faithful. Through Bible studies, testimonials and life examples, she had demonstrated to her young granddaughter the worth, dependability and the reality of the Love of God. But try as she might, Kitty just couldn't believe in God or His love for her. Now, *grandmother had just one more plan.*

Gently pushing Kitty away from her, Grandmother softly whispered as if realizing that Someone Else was in the room, *"Yea though I walk through the valley of the shadow of death I will fear no evil. Thy rod and thy staff they comfort me."*

The young charge looked at her aging mentor and experienced more than a twinge of exasperation. She couldn't help that she didn't believe as her grandmother wanted and prayed that she would. When Kitty surveyed the world that she lived in, she could see no evidence that God (if indeed He existed) cared anything about her or her grandmother. Why had He allowed her father and mother to get a divorce? Then, as if that wasn't enough, her mother died in a hotel fire and her father was killed in an automobile accident three months later. All this happened when she was seven years old. So, why should she believe in a God Who evidently didn't care about her?

Kitty didn't want to get into an argument with her grandmother but she had heard that the attack tonight was going to be the worst of the war so far.

"Grandmommy, *please come with me*! I know you believe in God *but you've got to use common sense!*"

She hadn't called her "Grandmommy" since she was ten years old. But somehow she felt so small and was so scared that the word just slipped out. Kitty took her grandmother by both of her hands, looked into her eyes and softly explained, "Grandmommy, I didn't want to tell you this earlier. Mr. Winters, at the butcher's shop on the corner said his son who works for the mayor said that he has it on good authority that this air raid will be the very biggest raid thus far in the war. There will be more planes dropping more bombs than at any time since the war started. *You just can't stay here!* I doubt that your God would want you to commit suicide!"

"No weapon formed against you shall prosper", the old grandmother replied again speaking as if she was reaffirming a truth to an Unseen Entity.

Frustrated and afraid, Kitty stood slightly bent forward at the waist in front of her grandmother. Her legs slightly apart, Kitty balled her fists up and hit her thighs, punctuating every word. She demanded angrily, "Stop quoting those old out of date verses from the Bible and come with me to the bomb shelter - *RIGHT NOW!*"

Her grandmother raised herself up in the rocking chair as tall as she could and with flashing eyes she spat out, "Kitty! Watch your mouth! *I'm still your grandmother*! Grandmother quickly lowered her voice and reasoned, "Listen, Baby Girl, I've trusted God and His Word for almost seventy years now and it's too late to start doubting Him now. My Bible says, *'If God be for you he is more than the world against you'*. So, Kitty, I'd much rather trust God than the bomb shelter. You go on now, Honey. And rest assured that the God I serve won't let me down!"

Just then, her best friend, Aresha, came from next door and peeked her head inside the screen door. "C'mon, girl, if you're coming!"

With a great sigh of defeat and frustration, the young granddaughter stared at her grandmother as if for the last time. She wanted to indelibly imprint the picture of her grandmother in her mind. She saw the old rocking chair that had been in its place long before Kitty had come to live at there. She saw her grandmother and the knitting needles and the sweater grandmother was knitting. She tried to stamp the image in her memory so surely that for the rest of her life she would see her grandmother as she now saw her. She wanted to remember her sitting tall in her rocking chair with the unfinished sweater in her lap and her knitting needles all but forgotten in her hands. She tried to memorize her grandmother with her kindly, piercing eyes filled with a purpose and a resolve that was so real that she was betting her life on them.

For a moment, the unfinished sweater gave Kitty cause to believe that her grandmother would be all right. Didn't she have to finish it? In the periphery of her mind she realized that she was being superstitious but she almost believed that the incomplete sweater would countermand fate and every other destiny planning entity that would orchestrate the death of the grandmother.

Kitty sadly shook her head in disappointment and disbelief. "How could you do this to me? You know that you are all I have in this whole world! *How could you do this to me?*" She sobbed as she ran out of the screen door and down the front steps.

The Great Facilitator knows that His agenda is never at risk. For He has stated, "My counsel shall stand, and I will do all my pleasure" (Isa 46:10 KJV) And again He promised, "I will hasten my word to perform it." (Jer 1:12 KJV) So, it is safe to say that the Lord knew what Kitty has yet to find out: that the plan of her grandmother's God will not fail! God will win in the end!

CHAPTER 15

WHO WAS REALLY ALONE?

It must be understood by all that God will go to great lengths to accomplish Divine Agenda! There are no lengths that he will not go to fulfill His purposes!

The two girls ran as fast as they could down streets that were almost deserted. They ran past the corner butcher shop where Mr. Winters had run out so fast that he'd forgotten to turn the lights off. Turning the corner, they shot past the bakery and the soda shop. Past the elementary school they ran. To Kitty, its emptiness seemed to be a harbinger of the doom she thought would surely fall tonight. "Strange how the streets look so ominous and foreboding!" the granddaughter mentally observed as she kept stride with her fleeing schoolmate, Aresha.

Aresha ran but not with the same mindset that Kitty had. Somehow, Aresha found it all so exciting. Aresha didn't have the sense of dread and fear that Kitty had. She felt an urgency to get to the bomb shelter - but for Kitty more than herself. Slowly it dawned on her that she felt a very real peace about her immediate future. "I'm so glad that I went up to the altar Sunday and gave my life to God," Aresha said to herself. "I'll never forsake my Savior and I know He will never desert me!"

They hit the double doors in full stride. Panting and gasping for breath, the two girls flopped down on one of the makeshift benches. They looked around in the semi darkness and saw all of their neighbors. The strain of the moment showed on every face. The sight of them was both comforting and alarming. Their appearance suggested that they were mostly unprepared for this evening flight for their lives. Mr. Winters, who had been cleaning his store for the next day's business still had his butcher's apron on. Mrs. Melodie Hanssen (who loved nothing more than working in the soil in the cool of the evening) still had her gardening tools in the pockets of her smock. She had been pruning and tending her prize roses. Little Amy Seals still had her toothbrush clutched tightly in her hand. She had been preparing for bed. Many of the smallest children were in various stages of being dressed for bed. And on it went with each person's attire or possessions giving some suggestion as to what he or she was doing the moment the siren sounded.

Aresha moved down to the farthest end of the bench and closed her eyes in prayer. "Dear Jesus, I just want to thank You for Your mercy and Your grace. I know that it's because You are so good to me that I am here, safe in Your arms. I know that if I die I'll just come straight home to You. Please, Lord, for the sake of all those who don't know You, I ask that You keep the bombs from hurting any of us. And, Dear Lord, I know You will keep Kitty's grandmother safe from harm.

Kitty looked over and saw Aresha opening her eyes. She couldn't help noticing that Aresha seemed newly possessed by an assurance and a confidence that was totally out of character for her. Everyone had talked much about the fact that Aresha had finally given her life to Christ. Secretly, Kitty envied the peace and joy that Aresha had or rather *the Peace and Joy that had Aresha.* Sometimes Kitty thought that she did believe in God but something always happened to make her doubt and wonder about Him (though she really wished she could believe).

Aresha moved back to sit near Kitty and put her arms around her. "Your grandmother will be all right, Kitty," she said.

"How can you be so sure? I mean, I never realized, 'Resha, how old she is before today. I feel so bad. I should have stayed with her to look after her. But I was just so afraid to die!' Kitty explained as she twisted the ends of her scarf.

"Oh, don't worry about her. Your grandmother will never be alone!" Aresha promised with a knowing look in her eyes.

The hope that drives and steadies the Watcher shall provide the privilege and the strength of mercy that will protect the unbeliever and keep him in the fight until the Grace of God enables the believer to develop confidence in the love and the compassion of the Lord, Jesus. You see, the mercy of God <u>denies the unbeliever what he justly deserves</u> while the Grace of God <u>provides the unbeliever with better than he deserves</u>. When the reward for sin is the immediate punishment of eternal death, Mercy shouts a stentorian, "No! Let him live!" However, despite the fact of the sinner not dying, the <u>sinner is not made better</u>

by mercy than he was before the condemnation! He is still precariously seated! Eternal Salvation is not his! He still must face a Just and Righteous God to give account for his sins. The Grace of God is different though, in that it places the penitent believer in a place of safety and security by giving him eternal life; meaning *better than he deserved*.

The manifested Presence of God enables the unbeliever to find *relief in*, and *deliverance from* and *victory over* the adversary. There are truly no better Watchers than "Hope, Grace, Mercy and the Presence and Love of God in one's life.

The Watchers in this story were multiple: 1) God Himself and "His Hope," 2) the Grace, Mercy and Love of God that the grandmother trusted in; 3) Aresha, who prayed for and encouraged her friend, Kitty. These all worked in tandem to insure the mental, spiritual and the physical wellbeing of Kitty and her grandmother and Aresha.

CHAPTER 16

LIVING POWER

*When you are filled with God's power you are never powerless!
There are times when the cost of being a Watcher is very high.
And one of the denominations that the currency is paid in is -
pride. The Watcher won't always be understood. However, when
the Watcher weighs the price of public acceptance against the cost
of compromising his vigil - there is no contest! The Watcher must
prove true to his watch.*

*There are no guarantees to the Watcher. Often, the Watcher
must bear the brunt of the unappreciative watched one's anger
and misunderstanding. To all whose judgments are founded in
reason that is just and wise, it will be apparent that the Watcher
doesn't guard to be popular or for the applause and accolades
from the watched one. Rather, it is the end result of successful
watching that is the lifeblood of the Watcher. The true Watcher
is on a sacred mission having a divine mandate.*

When Kitty and Aresha ran out of the house the loving
grandmother couldn't help herself. The tears just welled up
in her eyes and overflowed in tiny rivulets down her cheeks.

She didn't blame Kitty for the harsh words. It was just that they hurt so much coming from her granddaughter. She understood that there was so much that Kitty just did not understand; so much she was just too young to know.

The bone weary grandmother sat in her chair by the window and stared out into the empty street. She could still hear in her mind and see with her mind's eye, the neighborhood children in the street playing soccer. In her thoughts the present moment faded and gave way to the memories of earlier that day. As she thought and relived the afternoon's goings on she began to doze off to sleep.

In an out of sleep, she was soon violently awakened by the sound of more bombers than she had ever heard! They were so loud that they shook the windows. The high pitched scream of the falling bombs struck a momentary fear in her heart. For the moment, she forgot who she was and Whose she was. She jumped up from her seat faster than she had moved in months. Gone were the effects of her arthritis and rheumatism. Grandmother didn't even feel the pain in her ankles and joints.

Before she knew what she was doing, Grandmother headed toward the backdoor. On her way through the living room as she headed for the kitchen, she passed the coffee table where her well used, well-worn Bible lay open. She paused just long enough to lovingly pick her favorite Book up. The effect of touching the Bible that had touched her for most of her life was as if someone had roped her with a lasso. She appeared to have been snatched back by the waist. She spun around and gently went to her knees in worshipful thanksgiving. Suddenly, the walls began to shake and pictures tumbled down behind the piano and the couch. The big gilded mirror that grandmother's deceased husband bought her forty years ago fell to the carpet with such a violent force that it was a miracle shards of glass were not propelled across the room. Grandmother held the Bible to her bosom and looked up to heaven.

"Dear Jesus, I know You are more than real. I am not afraid. I know these German bombers cannot destroy me without Your Divine permission. However, Lord, it is for my little Kitty that I am praying. I'm not asking that You just spare my life but that You do it in a way that *Kitty will know beyond any shadow of doubt that You did it*! I thank You in advance because I am fully confident that as You have always done, You will answer my prayer. I ask this in precious name of Jesus."

All of a sudden, the whole world seemed to explode as the ground tossed and churned for what seemed like a full three minutes. The earth quaked as if to be shaken from its axle. The linoleum floor seemed to struggle to stay in one piece. Then she felt it! There was a Power in the room that could only have been – Him! The loudness of the war: the almost immeasurable volume of decibels that thousands of pounds of bombs coupled with the sound of houses falling in and buildings blowing up was all but totally eclipsed by the sheer wall of silence that filled the grandmother's house. She knew the exact moment that the Arms of Jesus wrapped themselves around her. She knew that she was not alone and also knew that she would never be *lonely* again. He was there! He wouldn't - No! He couldn't forsake her! The peace that flooded her heart was both forceful and tender, both comforting and caressing while it held her. It assured and promised her; filled her and fulfilled her; gave her joy and rejoicing.

Grandmother knew that most of the block her house was on must have been blown to bits. Clouds of dust filled the air and she could barely breathe. Holding the bottom of her apron to her nose, she clutched the Bible as if it was a divine tether that anchored her to her faith. She was strangely calm in the midst of the greatest confusion she had ever known.

Then she realized that the last salvo must have been the finale for she heard the sound of the bombers fading into the distance. The quiet that was left was, to her, as loud as the bursting bombs. She never before knew that she could hear silence! It was such a contrast to the sound of death that threatened the end of her life and the world as she knew it. Not only did she experience the audible sound of the silence but also she felt a calm as physically as she had ever felt anything in her life.

Grandmother picked herself up with feeling of gratitude that she could not put in words. All she could do was embrace the Bible with a desire to force it into her bosom; into her heart. She had never known her Savior as intimately as she now did. Somehow, she knew that should the whole world fall apart; should the whole world be annihilated she would ever be safe - in His Arms!

She went to the screened back porch and got the broom and her dusting cloth. Starting at the front of the house, she began to clean and dust. Carefully picking up the mirror, she didn't stop cleaning until the house was spotless.

She then went to bed full knowing that she would never again fear anything.

Early the next morning, as was her way, she woke up and thanked her Lord for keeping her through the night. Then she washed her face and hands, brushed her teeth and dressed herself. Finally, she went into the kitchen and began to prepare a very special breakfast. For she knew that this would be an eventful morning; it would be a most special day.

Quite often, as a fringe benefit of being a Watcher, the loving heart of God provides that during the course of watching, the Watcher is thrust to a new height and depth of intimacy, trust and understanding of the Lord. Kitty's grandmother was given a more than renewed sense of reliance on and assurance of the love of her Lord. Her heart was indelibly sealed with a complete knowledge of God's Love and a perfected strength of faith. This new found gift was not just a product of her emerging victoriously from her confrontation with death but was in a greater sense the result of the journey as she endured the ordeal!

CHAPTER 17

LORD, IF YOU WILL THEN I WILL

God's determination to save as many sinners as He can is clearly demonstrated by Him playing the "If – Then" game with man. The game goes like this: God says to man, "If you will obey my Will then I will bless you!" He could have simply said, "Give Me what I want or die"! But, wanting to be chosen, He renders to man one of the highest honors He has ever bestowed on mankind – the power of choice! Thusly He deals with Kitty in this chapter.

Kitty had been up pacing the floor while mentally arguing at her absent grandmother. Grandmother had always been the pillar of strength that Kitty could depend on. Now Kitty was sure that she would have no one left. What would she do now? An orphan! No family! Only an all knowing God could have known how to be this mean! And Grandmother expected her to love Him!

Finally, Kitty began to think about this Jesus in Whom Grandmother placed so much confidence. Who was this He anyway? *What* was He that people believed in Him almost two thousand years after He died? And how could she still believe in a God *Who took her daughter away* in the prime of her young adult life? But believe in Her Grandmother did! And not only does she believe in Him – *she loves, honors and obeys Him!* Kitty felt herself shudder violently. Though there was no movement of air in the shelter, she was cold. She looked around in the semi darkness. The lone forty-watt light bulb cast an eerie glow on the room. There seemed to be more shadows than lighted areas.

"What peace she always has!" soliloquized Kitty. So deep was she in her thoughts that she was unaware that anyone was listening to her. She added, "Maybe I've been wrong all the time. Perhaps Grandmother's Jesus is all that He is cut out to be."

Full knowing the gravity of her decision, Aresha was suddenly aware of a flash of thoughts in her mind. Just the beginning of a notion it was; they were just so many separate thoughts that had not yet become ideas she could act on. These hints that were at the brink of becoming ideas had come together as so many pieces of a puzzle. In a flash the phenomenal idea had become a purpose! As if to capture the idea before it could elude her, Kitty exclaimed aloud, "If grandmother has been in any real danger and her Jesus kept her, I vow that He will be my Jesus too - *for the rest of my life!*"

Aresha squeezed her hands tightly together and knew that all that had occurred this night was really God's plan for saving her friend. When she heard Kitty make her promise to God, Aresha felt her eyes well up with teardrops. She felt her face warm as the briny fluid first snaked from beneath her eyelids and then flooded down her face. "Lord, You are so good to us," observed Aresha. "Thank You for loving Kitty. I know You are going to save her!" Unwilling to break into Kitty's private musing, Aresha remained still and heard Kitty tell God," Father, if you convince me that You kept Grandmother in a miraculous way, I truly want you to give me the same kind of trust in You that Grandmother that You gave to my grandmother!

It was hard for Aresha to see her friend in such agony but she knew that out of the great pain great comfort would come. From the great confusion would emerge confidence and an understanding that that would never betray Kitty? She found herself wondering how anyone could doubt the reality of the Love of God.

It was impossible to tell that on the other side of the double doors the sun was just coming up. The bombs had stopped falling a long time ago. But Kitty couldn't understand why the "all clear" signal had not been given yet. She could hardly wait to get home to see if indeed Grandmother's God had spared her. She knew that her city had never been bombed like this before. It sounded like the battle of Armageddon! Surely very little would be left standing.

Kitty scarcely realized that she had been up all night. She sat on the far right end of the hard bench. It was as far away from the light as she could get. He fingers were tired and swollen from the twisting and squeezing that she nervously did all night long.

Finally, she heard it! The signal that declared the bombing threat was over! She jumped off the bench and ran to the double doors. Mr. Winters was trying to unlock the main one. But the old latch wouldn't act right. The pause gave her time to reflect on the possibilities of the bombing's aftermath. "What if Grandmother is dead?" she asked herself. "What if she is buried under the rubble that used to be our house?" What if Grandmother is at this moment lying with her body broken and bleeding, crying for help?

Without her knowing what it signified, Kitty quickly asserted, "No! I don't believe that God would let anything bad happen to Grandmother. He loves her too much!"

Just about that time the door latch came loose. Kitty threw the door open and hit the sidewalk in a full run. She vaguely heard Aresha yell, "Hey, Kitty! Wait up!"

Kitty never even slowed until she came to the elementary school. With a gasp of fright, Kitty saw that half of the school was leveled to the ground. There was a large crater where the front of the school used to be. Kitty thought it was very strange that she should remember how the principal of the school put so much emphasis on the kids walking on the sidewalk. "If you stay off the grass – the grass will last!" was his favorite saying. The bombed out school gave rise to a new level of fear for her grandmother. And without realizing it Kitty balled her fists up and pumped her arms and legs faster as she put on a burst of speed. The soda shop was a blur to her as she fairly *flew* past it. She saw to her dismay that the bakery was missing the whole chimney side of the building. Flying past Mr. Winter's butcher shop, Kitty saw the light still on. The knowledge that the butcher shop was still intact fueled Kitty with a newfound hope for her Grandmother.

Most of the run home would remain a blur to her for the rest of her life. The blocks that Kitty had to run from the butcher shop were run as if on automatic pilot. She just knew she was headed toward home.

When she finally arrived at her block, she saw smoke and rubble everywhere. Kitty slowed down in her surprise at the devastation the bombs had wrought. The big beautiful home of Dr. Warner was gone. All that was left was the big Oak tree that stood in the front yard next to the driveway. She saw little seven-year-old Joyce Ann Warner standing with her parents where their porch used to be. She was holding what was left of her dollhouse.

Kitty was unable to see her house that was at the far end of the block because of the steep hill in the middle of the block. Kitty began running again! She ran past houses that had windows broken, chimneys newly cracked and roofs caved in. She grew more and more frantic as she saw devastation and ruin on every hand. There was not one house that was in the same condition as before the bombing. Fallen trees damaged even cars and trucks. Many vehicles had windows that were shattered by the force of bombs that exploded too close. Gaping holes made the streets an obstacle course.

Breathing with loud gasps through her mouth, Kitty reminded God of the pact that she had covenanted with Him. "I promise, Lord, if you have worked a miracle and saved my grandmother's life, I will never doubt You again.

The Watcher has a wonderful tool to use in the business of Watching! It is the Will and the Way of God! Did you notice that Aresha knew just when to speak clearly to Kitty as well as when to back off and just give her a nudge now and again? And don't forget the timely prayers that Aresha prayed; prayers of petition and prayers of praise in anticipation of victory! The Watcher is there not to live the life of the watched one but to act as a facilitator, a reminder and sometimes a director. In this chapter, Kitty has done that job admirably!

Chapter 18

BECAUSE GOD DID – I WILL

It is not unlikely that God may step in and do the "hands on Watching!" When the bombs were falling and exploding all night long, there was no one but God on duty! It was He alone, Who directed or redirected the trajectory or the aim of the bomb! It didn't matter whether Satan sent a bomb to Grandmother's house or whether the devil blew the wind that propelled the bomb toward Grandmother's house or a human enemy targeted Grandmother's house – God Protected His faithful Child!

Finally, Kitty was almost home. She could now see to the other end of the block. Her heart nearly burst with joy as she saw that at least the front of her house was still standing. As she neared the house she slowed down to a nervous trot and then to a walk. Then she stopped! Standing there in amazement, she could scarcely believe her eyes! The whole house was still standing! And what was most incredible was the fact that in contrast to the rubble that the houses on both sides of her had been reduced to - *her Grandmother's house looked the same as it always had*! Not one thing was wrong!

Not one pane of glass was even cracked! Not one brick was out of place!

Then Kitty looked up at the roof and saw smoke coming from the chimney. It was then that she smelled the bacon, fried eggs, fried tomatoes, toast, sausages and beans. And she knew that the water for tea was heating on the stove. She ran into the house calling, "Grandmommy! Grandmommy! Did God keep you safe? Graaanmommy!"

Her grandmother came out of the kitchen wiping her hands on her apron as Kitty had seen her do a thousand times or more. There was a touch of flour on her nose as Grandmother smiled at Kitty. The silvery gray bun that was Grandmother's hairstyle coupled with the love and warmth of Grandmother's smile made Kitty swell with a sense of belonging and home. But the greatest wonder of all was that *Grandmother acted as if nothing out of the ordinary had occurred all night long.*

"Good morning," Kitty. "Glad to see you made it home. Go on in the bathroom and wash up now before your breakfast gets cold," Grandmother said. Kitty heard that warm gentle voice that always spelled "home" to her. She never knew that just the sound of a voice could so completely embrace her. But at that moment she felt all of her Grandmother's love wrap her up and squeeze her ever so tightly. She had always known that she loved her Grandmother but at this moment, she seemed possessed by the love to a greater degree than she had ever thought possible. Her love was so real that Kitty almost felt it tangibly.

Grandmother never even brought up the fact that Kitty spent the night in the bomb shelter. She knew that the Lord had dealt with Kitty all through the night. There was no doubt in Grandmother's mind that a major change had taken place in her grandchild. So, Grandmother could not help but sneak a glance as Kitty walked past her to go into the bathroom that was just off the kitchen. The bathroom door closed softly behind her but reopened more softly a moment later. Kitty surreptitiously put her head out and peeked at her Grandmother. She looked quizzically at her mentor and guardian. Then, closing the door gently, Kitty could only marvel at the tranquility and perfect harmony that her Grandmother had with the events of the previous night.

Kitty turned the water on and ran it until it was hot. Picking up her face cloth and the bar of soap, she couldn't help but remember the chaos and the danger that had characterized her world just a few hours ago. She shut her eyes and heard again the screaming whistle of the falling bombs. Giving an involuntary shudder as she relived their bursting impact, she could almost feel the ground shake beneath her. The acrid smell of the bombs, accompanied by the unmistakable odor of wood and rubber burning, still held back the odor of life, as Kitty knew it. It also lent to Kitty's reverie a genuine sense of reality and made the smell of breakfast and home in her Grandmother's house all the more peculiar and somewhat incongruent. The cold and loneliness of her previous night seemed to permeate the bathroom as, in her mind's eye, Kitty saw the still forms of her neighbors sleeping fitfully in their common bedroom – the bomb shelter. She still found it so hard to believe the terrible tragedy that all of her neighbors had suffered.

Kitty had not, for a moment, forgotten the unresolved issue between her and God. There was no doubt in her mind that a notable miracle had occurred in terms of her Grandmother having escaped injury and death from the bombing. It was also apparent to Kitty that the Lord had spared their home.

Her gratitude to God was more than she could express. But she wanted to calm herself and commit herself to developing a relationship with Him. When she closed the bathroom door, kitty leaned back against it and whispered, "Lord, You have been so good to Grandmother and for that I want serve You for the rest of my life. However, I truly need You to demonstrate to me that You will be a *personal* Savior to me. I am convinced that You are the True God. And I am certain that you love my Grandmother. But I just have to know that I can trust You to be the *Personal Savior and Friend that I need*. I mean, the way I see it, You have never been there for me! You did after all, let my Dad and Mother die!" Without realizing what she was doing, Kitty soaped the cloth and began to wash her face. Then she rinsed the towel and wiped her face. Next, Kitty reached to place her wash cloth on the towel rack. Suddenly, she was startled by her own reflection in the mirror. She paused in mid wipe. There was no difference in her physical countenance. Her hair was still the same jet-black color and her eyes had not changed. They were still almond shaped and hazel in color. Her high cheekbones that Grandmother had always said, "gives your face character," were still a mark of beauty.

But something very strange was happening! The face she was focusing on was not the face she washed yesterday morning nor was it the face she expected to see this morning. The face that looked back at her in the mirror was *her own face when she was just seven years of age.* She knew instinctively that she was seeing herself on the day of her mother's funeral. She saw her eyes swollen and red from crying. Somehow, through the mirror and across the years, she saw herself as she had stood before this same mirror after she and her grandmother had come home after the graveside ceremony. Kitty remembered how small, alone and empty she had felt after everyone had gone home.

She also remembered how no one knew how to say what she needed to hear. Everyone said the same things. "Don't cry. Your mother has gone to a better place." Things like that. Why couldn't they all just understand that her mother's place was with her? Surely, there is no better place for a mother than with her daughter! Kitty remembered thinking, "At what age do grownups stop needing their mother and father? I will never ever get so old that I don't need my mommy and my daddy!" vowed Kitty.

Ever so slowly, the image in the mirror began to change. Soon she saw herself in her bedclothes. She recognized that the image in her mirror was of her lying in her bed. She recalled that in the middle of the night she had cried in her sleep so loudly that she woke herself. Now, Kitty saw herself sit up in the bed with a heart filled with sorrow and fear. She remembered wondering who would be next to die. Will it be her Grandmother? *I know it will be somebody!* Who will it be? Will it be me?

Somehow, because of these wonderful reminders of how God had been in her life and in such a personal way, when she had needed Him the most – she knew that He would be there for her for the rest of her life *and even beyond into the final eternity!*

Unlike so many who come to Jesus, Kitty realized that she needed a savior but she also knew that she needed a PERSONAL SAVIOR! Kitty didn't just want a God Who lived way up there in Heaven somewhere – she needed a God who would be there for her; like after the graveside service and Who would be there and care and understand when she could not stop the tears and when the heartaches of life wouldn't go away! She needed the God that she had forgotten He could be!

CHAPTER 19

THE MAN IN THE MIRROR

Isa 46:9-10: "…I am God, and there is none else; I am God, and there is none like me, <u>declaring the end from the beginning, and from ancient times the things that are not yet done, saying, My counsel shall stand, and I will do all my pleasure.</u>" (KJV)

The Omniscient Heart of God coupled with his Omnipotent Power is the Authority that enables the true believer to know a consummate peace of mind and enjoy perfect rest in body no matter the stress. For, it is the All Knowing and the all Powerfulness of God that orchestrates and defends the believer in this world. God sees and knows our future because He designs our future! In that He is already in our future He knows what He must place there for our sustaining, maintain and our prosperity!

In this chapter you will witness, first hand, the preparedness of our Savior Who provides for our needs before we need His preparations!

Reliving the experience, Kitty knew the moment when she suddenly sensed that she had not been alone in the bedroom that day seven years ago. In the room with her had been the Gentlest of Men. He was the most wonderful and understanding Person she had ever met. He had looked at her with eyes that made all the answers to her questions totally unnecessary. The compassion and the love that was in those eyes made trust an automatic and feel-right thing. She didn't know who He was but she knew that He would never hurt her and that she was completely safe with Him.

He smiled and all the darkness melted out of her heart. All of her mind wrenching sorrows, fears and torments completely left her and her loneliness was not even a distant memory. That smile did it; that smile that made her *feel* so much more than she *saw*. That wonderful smile promised, "You will cry no more tonight!" That smile! That smile was in itself an assurance that the Man would stay there as long as she needed Him that night. She knew that He would be with her all night if necessary!

Kitty could not tear herself away from the mirror. She watched the drama unfold in the mirror just as it had that day when she was seven years old. She watched

her up in His arms. He walked over to her bed and sat on the side of the bed holding her. He held her as if she was the greatest treasure in His life.

She lay there for a while relaxing and enjoying the music that was lulling her to a deep and rest-filled sleep. Almost without her realizing that she was doing it, Kitty had examined the melody for its source. As she leaned her head against Him, she had heard the sound of the most beautiful and peaceful ever so calming music. It was quiet in her ears and more than that it was quieting to her spirit. As a child of seven years, she had not known how to define the difference between this and any other music she had ever heard. But the truth is - the unique musical phrases and rhythmic patterns were unlike any she had heard before. The music seemed to invite her to listen but at the same time the sound was so satisfying and so fulfilling that it made attentive listening unnecessary. Indeed, it was as if she didn't have to focus on hearing it. The living sounds made themselves heard. Listening now, Kitty understood that for the first time in her young life she had experienced *the audible sound of love.* She had often *felt* love. She had *seen* love offered but never had she even imagined that *love could be actually heard.* With her head against His chest, she could hear His heartbeat. With absolute certainty, Kitty knew that the music that so filled her heart and fulfilled her soul *was simply and profoundly - the beat of His tender and loving heart.*

He didn't say anything. He didn't have to. His Presence was all fulfilling! The music was filled with melodies and counter melodies. She never thought of the music as a song. It was more like phrases that assured her soul that the Love of God was hers to possess. The counter melodies intertwined with the melodies and gave reassuring confirmation that all of the Love of God was indeed at her disposal. There were no lyrics sung but the notes, the chords and rhythm patterns created words in her heart, soul and mind that expressed to her all the love that God had ever had for her. The more the music caressed her, the more deeply and clearly she understood the depth of His great affection for her.

Kitty *now* understood so many things that she hadn't realized seven years before. Somehow, she now knew that the Divine purpose for her experience with Jesus that so comforted her on the day of her mother's funeral was to simply and completely comfort her *then*. But the Multi-tasking Love of God had also purposed that Kitty would, seven years later, have this mirror experience! Jesus had planned to satisfy Kitty's every emotional and spiritual need *then* but also included her needs on this day seven *years later!* He knew it would take His Perfect Love to perfect her love for Him.

During the times that immediately followed the passing of her mother and then her father, Kitty endured some things that had had not made any sense to her.

At the time of this wonderful mirror experience, Kitty did not realize the mechanics of the whole healing and satisfying process. But she was now sixteen years old as she stared transfixed into the mirror. Being older and wiser, she was able to understand more fully what before she had accepted as just the way things happened.

Somehow, the question that had lingered in the back of her mind from time to time was finally answered. She only just now realized Who the Man was. He was Jesus! At long last, Kitty knew that Jesus was real and had been concerned about her all of her life.

As the young teenager looked into the mirror, Jesus turned his face directly toward Kitty. The look that was in His eyes was the same tender, soul caressing gaze that she remembered from that day so long ago.

Though she knew that she was looking at events that happened years ago, she marveled that even then He had known that one day she would stand before the same looking glass. He had known way back then she would need Him again to calm her fears and make her to know her worth in the heart of God.

Kitty was fully aware that on that day, when she was seven years of age, there was no one He could look at when He gazed directly into the mirror. Her mind and heart were full of marveling at the awesome understanding and the all-knowing of God. Though she did not know the words to express the ideas even to herself, the reasoning was building and growing in her that *seven years ago He knew that seven years later to the exact day and time He would be looking at her through the looking glass!*

As Jesus looked into her eyes, she knew a strangely familiar comfort and solace. She felt warm and all aglow when saw Him give the faintest whisper of a wink and just the shadow of a smile. The small gesture was so personal and so intimate that it was more than enough to make Kitty understand that *this moment in time was planned many years before!*

Slowly, gently, so as to not leave kitty with the sense of being left or abandoned, the images in the mirror and the music began to fade until Kitty could only see the reflection of her sixteen-year-old self.

Feeling so loved by the calm that she felt, Kitty spoke aloud to the same Jesus that she had only hours before distrusted with so much vehemence and anger.

"Oh, dear Jesus, I am so sorry that I took so long to remember You. For, now, I do remember You. I remember when You were the only One to care *and* understand me. Lord, I want to spend the rest of my life serving You and telling everybody I know about You. I want You to fill me with Your Holy Spirit and use me for Your work for the rest of my life."

Kitty hung the face cloth across the towel rack and walked out of the bathroom. Breakfast was waiting for her on the table. She sat down and her Grandmother sat down with her.

"Granny, can I ask you a question?'

"Sure, baby," replied Grandmother.

"I didn't get one minute of sleep last night. Did you sleep at all?"

Grandmother looked at Kitty with eyes that reflected great and experience bought wisdom and answered, "Kitty, I knew that the Lord was going to stay up all night and watch over us. So there was no need for both of us to lose our sleep!"

"Grandmother," Kitty said. "If you don't mind, I would like to ask God's blessing on the food this morning."

Grandmother, with tears of joy filling her eyes, simply nodded her head as if this was the most natural thing in the world for her Granddaughter to ask. And, indeed it was! For, Grandmother truly believed God.

When God, the Ultimate Watcher, is on duty, and He always is, the Watched one never needs fear for tomorrow because God is already there! Actually, neither the one who was Watched or the Watcher needed to fear because God has infinitely better than perfect timing! In our lives as human beings we have on occasions commended a person for having perfect timing! By this we mean that the person came on time. God, However, has a timing that is far better than man. For, according to Isaiah 65:24, God

Promised: "And it shall come to pass, that before they call, I will answer; and while they are yet speaking, I will hear". (KJV) Note that in this story, Jesus prepared for His intervention years before Kitty needed it!

CHAPTER 20

THE INCOMPARABLE LOUISE

The need for strong character and high self-esteem in our society is great. Low self-esteem and weak character is a powerful detriment to one living a successful and noble life. The desire to belong and the need to fit in can be catalysts that cause some people to go against the norms and the mores of decent folk and can result in one actually committing crimes to get what they want. If this kind of flaw is a part one one's nature, it's like one being one's own "Trojan horse." One has then to fight the enemy within oneself!

Louise, the principle character in this story had nobody to Watch over her to ensure that she thought well of herself. She had no Watcher in this regard so she had to be her own Watcher. She built a wall of both pride for her present day living, and hope for her future. This veneer of strong sense of self was developed and strengthened daily as she proved to everyone around that she was and will ever remain, "The Incomparable Louise!"

I remember it as if it were yesterday though in reality it happened almost sixty years ago. The evening was warm.

The moon not yet out. It was as if the moon was afraid for its silvery light to be compared to the brilliance of the summer sun of one of the hottest days that year. I was sitting on the porch remembering what fun the Posse (our neighborhood fellows) and I had enjoyed that day.

I still grin inwardly as I see, in my mind, the sight that about bowled me over with laughter at the street shower earlier that day. Every Saturday from noon 'til 2:00pm the city would block both ends of Clinton Street between Dubois and St. Aubin and turn the fire hydrant on. We kids could play in the water and cool off.

Everybody was having a good time shoving one another in front of the hydrant and trying to see who could stand closest to the hydrant without being pushed down or knocked back by the force of the water.

Just as the fun was really getting started, Louise, Junebug's youngest sister, came out of the house. Now, everybody knew that Louise thought she was the prettiest girl on the block. She was always putting on airs and primping in front of everybody. She claimed that her hair was the prettiest and her dresses the most beautiful in our school.

Nobody could guess whom she would imagine herself from one day to the next but we all knew that she was the boniest little girl in the neighborhood. She would have been a nice friend and most of the kids would have liked her but she pushed people away with her arrogant attitude. She probably hadn't meant to be arrogant and prideful, rather, as I review her character in retrospect, she was almost certainly only living the character of one of her Hollywood personas. The thing is that while we all needed one another to validate us,

Louise needed no one. She was forever and always the grand and elegant LOUISE!

Whenever she saw a movie in which the star was a girl, she became that girl. She would see herself as that girl until someone else on the movie or television screen impressed her. At one time she was acting and talking like she was Shirley Temple. The problem was her short hair wasn't long enough to make the famed curls and her hair surely wasn't blond. But that didn't stop her from going around tap-dancing all of the time. It was hilarious to watch! Her spindly little legs looked like somebody tied knots in them to make her knees.

I didn't mind that she thought she was a movie star and beautiful and all. But what I didn't like most was that she kept telling everyone that she was "in luuuuve with Buddy." Plus, the way she said "luuuuve" by just dragging the word out so everybody would believe that she was truly in love was more than I could stand; and she was just seven years old? Yep, you guess it! My name is Buddy and Louise was much too young for me! I was twelve!

I can still see Louise when she first stepped out on the porch of her house that day. My mouth dropped open and all I could do was stare. Louise had tied a plastic cleaner's bag on her hair for a bathing cap and had on a two-piece bathing suit. The bathing suit belonged to her older sister, Lois. In order to make the bikini fit, Louise had stuffed the chest of the bikini with pieces of toilet paper. Now, nobody knew at that time that she had toilet paper in her bikini. But it turned out that she didn't just stuff her bikini top with toilet paper but she also filled the bottom of her bathing suit with it as well!

I remember seeing the biggest chest anybody had ever seen on a seven-year old girl! But to see those knobby kneed little legs sticking out from under the largest bottom a skinny little girl ever had was just too hilarious. I can still see her homemade chest sticking out over her skinny body! Her bony hips jutted out and appeared bonier when she tried to walk with what she thought was a very mature swaying. Her hips didn't sway like I am sure she meant them to they just jerked to the left and jerked to the right. She really believed that she was God's gift to the world.

Louse did her best to glide down the steps from her porch. When she stepped to the ground, she stepped into a puddle of muddy water from the fire hydrant. When I saw the gymnastics that she did to keep her balance - I almost lost it! The most important thing to Louise was that she maintained her dignity. That was impossible to do while she was flailing her arms and trying to keep from going down into the mud. I've got to give it to her though. Only Louise could have pulled it off. She never went down. Her little legs went every which way and her arms waved in directions that I never knew they could at the same time.

Now, Junebug loved his sister and would fight to defend her at the drop of a hat. But even he couldn't help but break up at the sight of Louise. When I saw him, he was going down to his knees laughing his head off! As a matter of fact, everybody at the street shower was laughing and pointing at Louise.

But Louise couldn't care less how everybody else saw her. She just sashayed across the grass toward the flowing water. Not really knowing how cold the water was, Louise stopped just short of the reach of the stream that was being pumped out into the street. Wobbles was standing in the flow of water using one hand to keep the water from snatching his swim trunks down. Suddenly, he reached over and grabbed Louise by one arm and pulled her into the water. She tried to act like she was going to get in the water anyway and squealed as she was half pulled and she half jumped into the shower. When that water hit her it almost knocked her over. She grabbed hold of Wobbles to keep her footing. Because the water hit her so hard she forgot to hold on to her bikini top and to her horror when she finally looked down at her chest she saw her top completely deflated. The water kept hitting her in the chest until we saw the white toilet paper all over the street and being sucked down into the gutter. When she saw what was happening to her chest, Louise turned around with her hands protecting her chest. But when she turned her back to the hydrant, the water did a job on the bottom of her bikini. The same force of water that had Wobbles holding his trunks up with one hand blasted Louise square on target. She must have had an entire roll of tissue in her bottoms. Now it was all out. Some was plastered to the side of her face. Some was in the street and some was even on Wobbles' stomach.

But you really had to know Louise to know that she would somehow maintain her dignity even in the face of this fiasco. I remember it clearly. Louise took her finger and put a big twist in the top of her bikini bottoms and secured them tightly at the waist. Then she held her head up high, squared her shoulders back and did her gliding thing out of the water and up the sidewalk to her house. She didn't look to the right or to the left. Her jaw was set and her eyes had a look that said she was still in control; she was still the elegant LOUISE!

Louise was probably destined to become someone great. For that day she made everyone know that there was more to her than met the eye. The way she refused to allow anything to cause her to see herself to any degree less than she valued herself said to all of us that she would never be defined by anyone *but herself!* And for as long as I knew her she was still the grand and elegant - LOUISE.

CHAPTER 21

"I AM MY FATHER'S SON"

Sometimes, those who have the potentials to be great and diligent Watchers are denied that privilege because the one who needs Watching will keep the need secret! This may be done out of a heart of pride; not wanting others to know that a vulnerability is present! Others seek to appear in control, provided for and safe because they are not able to trust others.

They were called "Blessed Acres." The sprawling, evenly cut acres were lush and perfectly maintained. One got the notion that on these grounds anything could be grown. The grand estate included a magnificent mansion that people came from all over to see. The Eden-like flower garden that bordered the house and lined the long winding driveway was legendary. The manor was complete with an Olympic size swimming pool, a sauna and a Jacuzzi, and a stable filled with high quality pure blooded show and pleasure horses. The property was a monument to landscaping and architectural genius. The fences provided grazing places for the yearlings and the brood mares. There was also a more than adequate riding ring. All the fences were gleaming white. The servant's quarters were a separate house than "The Great House" (as the servants called the mansion). The driveway circled in front of the Great House. A large and beautifully ornate white fountain stood in the middle of the circle.

The mansion was filled with light. The chandeliers, lamps, the walls, the pictures, the furniture and even the carpet on the floors, all created an atmosphere of light and there was an aura of gladness. The servants in the house worked in concert to provide a setting that contributed to happiness, security and peace. The crowning touch of this domestic masterpiece, however, was the family that brought all the other elements of the mansion together in a warm and loving tapestry of family, home and success. Indeed, it was the family that made all this potential – *a home.*

First, there was the father. He was a kind and generous, patient and loving man. He lived for his lovely wife and was devoted to their only son, Junior – the apple of his eye. His gentle voice was always ready to speak words that were seasoned with wisdom, mixed with understanding and ready with a humor that somehow caused every problem to be no more than an opportunity for a victory.

The woman of the manor, who was the essence of all that is gracious, gave real life to the words, "wife" and "mother." She was both a lady and a woman in the pure sense of each word. She loved her husband and responded to his love while she also respected and appreciated him. She nurtured and loved their only son. She was the perfect mother.

It appeared that there was nothing that this family lacked. Indeed, they both strengthened one another and sought to find strength in one another. However, *there was something missing!* The father noticed it and the mother felt it at just about the same time.

Their son, Junior, who was a faithful and loving child, usually so happy and fulfilled, was gradually growing sadder and more withdrawn each day. Hugs from his parents didn't affect him as they had in times past. His father's humor couldn't even cause him to smile. When his mother embraced him his whole world usually got brighter - but not anymore!

He was not happy! Junior wasn't angry. He just wasn't happy. He didn't ride his bike anymore nor play his video games. His books were now uninteresting and the television was boring to him. No matter the menu, he didn't have an appetite. He didn't want to visit his many friends and didn't want them to visit him.

"Junior is so unhappy that he won't eat. But the doctor says there is nothing physically wrong with him," the mother told her husband when he came home after work one evening.

"I know! I see it too!" the father replied. "I asked him what's wrong but he wouldn't say. Come on, Honey! We've got to find out what the problem is now!"

They went out to the backyard where Junior was sitting on the swing. He wasn't swinging. He was just sitting on the swing. The boy didn't even seem to notice them until his mother spoke to him. "A penny for your thoughts," she said

He looked up in surprise and said, "Hi, Mom, Hi, Dad."

"What's the matter, Son", the father asked, his voice was filled with concern.

"Oh, I'll be all right, Dad," he answered off handedly.

"Come on now, Junior, your mother and I are worried about you. Let me ask you something, Junior. Why can't you trust us?"

The ten-year-old looked into his father's face to see if he was joking. Realizing that his father was serious, he looked from him to his mother and answered, "I do trust you - more than anyone I know! What makes you think I don't trust you?"

"Well, Love," his mother explained, "When something is bothering you so much that you don't want to eat and you can't talk to us about it what should we think?"

The boy dropped his chin down on his chest. "Aw, Dad, Mom, I know how much you love me and I love you too. But that's why I just couldn't tell you what's wrong. I've been trying to forget it but I just can't get it out of his mind."

The father couldn't wait any longer. "You can't get *what* out of your mind?" He demanded.

"Dad, I know that the doctor said if Mom had another baby it could kill you. But, Mom, Dad, I want a brother! I know how selfish that is and that's the reason I didn't want to tell you! I have really been trying to forget it but I can't! It's in my thoughts. I even dream of playing with a brother. Dad, I love playing ball with you and video games and all but I just wish I had a brother to play with and talk to. And Mom, no one should ask for more than you give me and I am so sorry that I want a brother – *but I do!*"

No one could have mistaken the look on the faces of his parents for anything but joyous surprise. For about a month, now, the loving parents had been talking about enlarging the family with another son. Knowing that it would be hazardous for his wife to try to have another baby, her husband had suggested that they adopt a boy. They both agreed that this is what they would do if their son approved of the idea.

"Junior, the mother said, "Your father and I have been trying to find a way to tell you that we have been wanting another boy in this family also."

"Yes, Son," the father added. "We just didn't want you to think that we are not satisfied with you. Rather, it's because we are so happy with you that we want another son!"

Junior could scarcely believe that he had been so worried over this. "You really mean it? I can really have a brother?" he exclaimed. "Oh! Dad and Mom you are the greatest parents in the whole world!"

The very next day the father made the phone call to his lawyer who got the paperwork rushed through. Within a week the appointment was made to go to the orphanage and choose a boy.

The family spent the whole week preparing for their new family member. New bunk beds were bought and for every toy that their first son had another toy was purchased for their new son.

They were so busy that the week went by seemingly in a flash – *all except the night before the adoption!* The whole household was finding it hard to settle down.

"What will his name be, Mom?" "How old will he be, Dad?" "Will he to my school?" "How big will he be?" And a myriad of other questions flowed from the happy little ten year olds lips.

The proud father and mother-to be just kept glancing at one another and smiling. It was almost as if they were having their first child all over again.

Finally, everyone went to bed to dream of a new son and a new brother.

How alike humankind is to one another! How often has mankind peeled back a layer of someone else's life, personality and character only to see a reflection of themselves and their concerns! The same need that worried and caused so much pain in Junior was visited upon his parents. If man would seek to complete one another, how often will man find his own satisfaction! How often would he find his own fulfillment!

CHAPTER 22

HE WAS WORTH "NIL"

How often have the greatest treasures been found in the most unlikely places! How many times has what had been labeled and given the unworthy assessment of fool's gold been discovered to be worth more than the most perfect and exquisite diamonds! That which is rejected in and because of ignorance may well be deemed of prime importance and of inestimable value by the wise!

The building was large and foreboding. The dark red brick looked a dirty brown in the murky blackness of the moonless night. Most of the front of the old orphanage was obscured by the towering oak trees and leafy maples. The old building was built about fifty years ago by the richest man in the town. He had died alone and lonely. Nobody knew if he had any family. And, whenever anybody talked about him, the point would be clearly made that he had known how to make a living but had never learned how to make a life.

The rumor was that he had never made a will because either he was too stingy to share his wealth or he just didn't know anyone he felt deserved it. But he had lived alone and he had died alone! It was almost as if he was the first orphan to live in the old house.

The mansion became an orphanage when the mayor and the city council voted that since and there was a need for a place to house and care for little orphan boys, the mansion would be used for just that purpose. Then they commissioned a statue to be made and erected it on the front lawn in the old man's honor.

The old statue was virtually lost in the shadows of the night. Already, the nocturnal birds and the sounds of the night were in evidence. The crickets were chirping their love calls and the old owl that had for so long lived in the attic (over what used to be the stable) softly hooted at unpredictable intervals. And little gray mice were just beginning their night long searches for food.

Officer Niles, the patrolman whose beat took him past the orphanage, was just now passing under the street lamp at the corner of the great wrought iron fence that surrounded the property. Swinging his night stick in cadence to the happy song he was whistling, the officer was totally unaware of how much his happy mood did not match the serious and dismal setting of the orphanage.

Inside the building, the lights were being turned off room by room (the older boys shared rooms that housed two boys per room) and dorm by dorm where all of the other boys lived. The time was nine o' clock; the time that all of the boys went to bed. As the Dorm Master went from room to room his shoes clicked loudly on the hardwood floors that the boys had to polish on their hands and knees every Saturday morning.

Under the cloak of darkness, a little ten-year-old boy relaxed more than he had all day. He breathed an audible sigh of relief. Small for his age, he was, and so frail! All day long he had been on his guard (not that he could really defend himself). He really didn't know how to fight and the boys bullied him unmercifully. He seemed always to be running or hiding from somebody. And many times he was bullied by two or three boys at one time.

He thought the guys would never go to sleep. But he knew why they were all too excited to go to sleep. No one knew who started the rumor but most believed it. And even those who didn't really believe it joined in the fun of the idea. Everybody was wondering if tomorrow *someone really was going to be adopted!*

Quietly reaching to the foot of the bed where his coveralls were draped, he got the two biscuits he had managed to hide in the cuffs of his two-sizes-too-big coveralls. He pulled the ragged blanket over his head to lessen the chance that one of the boys in the cots on either side of his would see or smell the biscuits and come over to his bed and take them. Biting off a chunk of one, the boy sucked on the hard bread until it got soft enough to chew without crunching.

This was somehow the highlight of his day. This was the one chance he'd gotten to fool them all. No one had seen him take the two extra biscuits and secret them in his pocket until he could go to the bathroom and hide them in his pants cuffs.

He smiled as he remembered just how he had sneaked his late night treat. He had seen the little mouse peek his furry head out of the hole in the wall just behind the Dorm Master's chair at the supper table. He'd watched as the little rodent scurried over to the table. It was quiet at the table. At least as quiet as it ever was. The Dorm Master never allowed any talking at the table and if he caught somebody talking he would make the talker stand behind his chair and watch all of the other boys eat their food. Then he would order the talker to throw his food in the garbage. Dinner was never a quiet affair though, because the Dorm Master was the noisiest eater the boys have ever seen! He was a hugely fat man and he breathed through his nose and mouth very loudly and grunted and groaned as he chewed his food! The more he enjoyed his food, the more noise he made!

All of a sudden the Dorm Master jumped up from the table, knocking his chair over and grabbed one leg of his pants. The mouse had crawled up his pants leg and who knows just what the little furry rodent was intending to do? Those pants came off so suddenly that the poor little mouse was flung across the room where he made a bee line under the door and out into the hall he went.

While all of the boys were looking at the Dorm Master in his red Long John underwear and doing their level best to keep a straight face, the little boy grabbed two of the biggest biscuits on the platter. That he wasn't discovered and now had the best snack he'd had in a long time somehow made up for all the bad things that had befallen him that day.

The following morning, last as always, the little boy got his tray and slowly walked through the breakfast line. The white corn meal mush and fried Spam had never looked or smelled good to the little guy before and this time was no exception. Quickly straightening his face from the grimace that seemed to take over his face all by itself, the ten-year-old held his tray up so Cook could slop the cereal on the plate and angrily slap the Spam on top of the grits. The little boy did not know why Cook was always so angry with him - *but wasn't everybody?*

The Dorm Master always made a big show of his relationship with God. He really acted like God was his and his alone. Though he never got around to letting God be seen *in* him by showing compassion and gentleness. The little boy thought that maybe it was enough to the Dorm Master that he be seen *talking to* God. The Dorm Master began to say the blessing over the breakfast with, "My Father, I thank Thee on behalf of these unworthy urchins who don't know You." All the orphans clearly heard the emphasis on the words "*My Father*" and "*I thank Thee.*" And nobody ever found out what "*urchins*" were.

The Dorm Master didn't eat the same food the orphans ate. Cook always prepared him a real breakfast of bacon and sausage, smothered potatoes, oatmeal, eggs, orange juice, coffee and toast.

In contrast to many of the other boys, the lad never thought that this was unfair treatment. It was just his life! He had never known any life but the life of the orphan and by this time he was truly an orphan in every sense of the word.

As he ate his breakfast, he heard the excited whispers of the most wonderful news. *Someone really was going to be adopted today!* He looked around. All of the boys at every table were grinning and eating and whispering to one another when the Dorm Master was not looking their way. The little tyke wondered in a kind of fleeting thought if today his dream would come true.

He loved dreaming because then he could be anyone he wanted to and go anywhere he wanted to go. He also loved to read and it was through the medium of books that he roamed the plains with Kit Carson and played in the jungle with Mowgli, the boy who was raised by the apes. He loved to go to his favorite dreaming place in the attic where no one ever went but him. He didn't mind the dust and cobwebs and even the occasional spider because he knew that it was for these things that nobody went up into his dreaming place. He would sit down in front of a small round window that overlooked the backyard. From there, among long forgotten crates, dressers, cardboard boxes and junk, he dreamed of being in all of those wonderful places he had read about. His favorite dream, though, was the one in which the old orphanage was a grand mansion again.

In his dreaming place, he always remembered a book he had read. In the book a rich family lived in a mansion. And a little boy his age was the son of the richest family in town. The mother of the little boy in the story was a very grand lady who went to grand balls and parties. She wore a beautiful hat with a long feather in it and white gloves. When she took her gloves off, the diamond rings, necklace and bracelets would outshine the sun with colors that would just dance in the light. She wore a long fur coat and high heel shoes, and she always smells so good.

The story also told of the little boy's father who was tall and straight and wore a hat such as gentlemen wear. His top hat and his long gray overcoat made him appear even taller than he was. His black-gloved hands held a walking cane with a real gold handle and his shiny black shoes never *ever* got dusty!

Of course, as the little orphan read the story, he imagined that he was that little boy and the mother and father were his adoptive parents. But, he knew that the story was just that, a story that had no place in the real world; it certainly had no place in his world!

"All right, you little urchins" (the Dorm Master always called them, "*You urchins*" when he was speaking to them), "It's time for you to get cleaned up for our guests! Get up and push your chairs back under the table! Then go upstairs and wash! Be sure to wash behind your ears and brush your teeth. Put on your best clothes and wipe the dust off your shoes! Hurry up, now! MOVE URCHINS!" he ordered.

Chairs screeched in painful dissonance, scraping harshly against the hardwood floor as they were pushed back from the tables. There was a mad scramble and yells as the boys finally knew for certain that the rumor was true. The boys ran out of the room "high-fiving" each other and declaring that it will surely be "me" who will be adopted. No one truthfully knew who it would be but they all knew that *somebody really was going to get adopted today*!

"Nil, you come here!" the Dorm Master ordered. "Nil" was a word that meant "zero". It meant "nothing!" For as long as the little orphan boy could remember, the Dorm Master had called him, "Nil." The youngster didn't know what the word meant but he felt bad because of the way the Dorm Master said, "Nil."

"Nil, you needn't go getting your hopes up because nobody will ever want to adopt a useless zero like you!" he said, scowling darkly. So you stay right here and sweep the dining room floor while the rest of the boys get ready to be presented to my guests!" Nil jumped out of the way just as the big foot came crashing down where his toes had been. He had been ready that time! The Dorm Master had made an evil game of trying to stomp Nil's toes whenever he finished talking to him. The Dorm Master looked at him with an evil hatred on his face that threatened to get him the next time. Turning on his heel, the Dorm Master stomped away.

Nil hated the fact that the Dorm Master was right; that he truly was not going to be adopted. His feelings were confirmed as he looked into the large mirror that hung over the mantle of the fireplace. He saw a little boy wearing a red and white striped tee shirt under a pair of dirty coveralls that had a button missing so one strap dangled. He saw a little boy whose feet were bare and scarred from many splinters and cuts; a little boy with a dirty face and uncombed hair; *a little boy who would never, no; a little boy who could never be adopted!*

Nil went to the broom closet and got the old straw broom and began to sweep the room. He wasn't sure if it was the dust at first that caused the tears to well up in his eyes. But well up they did! Pretty soon Nil could barely see the floor through the hot tears that by now were flooding down his cheeks.

"What's the matter with me? Why is everybody else better than I am?" Nil asked himself. "Why was I even born?" Nil was sweeping furiously now. Dust was swirling in the air and covering everything. The windows were open to let an occasional breeze into the room and dust was always a problem. But, Nil didn't care right now! He wasn't sweeping the floor. He was trying to hit back at everything that had ever hurt him. He was sweeping Dorm Master away! He was sweeping the bullies away! He was sweeping the nightmares away! *He was sweeping his miserable life away!*

Chapter 23

"DREAMS REALLY DO COME TRUE"

There are actually people in this world who can give what they believe is true evidence of their worthlessness! There are those who have bought into the notion that <u>they were born to adversity</u>! I say, "There <u>should</u> be a Watcher for them!" I declare that, "There <u>must</u> be a Watcher for these hapless souls"! And I know as surely as I know the Love of God is real that <u>There is a Watcher for them</u>!

"Line up around the walls!" the Dorm Master commanded for the umpteenth time. He was in all of his Hitler-like glory. He strutted around barking orders like he was a drill sergeant. His more than ample stomach was bulging out so far that the buttons on his vest were threatening to pop off.

"I said line up! They'll be here any minute!" Every time he spoke, he punctuated his words with a finger poke to some little fellow's chest or a slap to the back of a head.

The night before, all of the dorms were abuzz with anticipation for the next morning. Each boy told the other kids what he would do to get the attention of the adopting couple. Each tried to outdo the other in planning his special performance.

Little Nil watched the circus-like scenario from his place in the corner. The Dorm Master had done all that he could to ensure that Nil would not be chosen. Left with a dirty face and hair uncombed, Nil had to stand in the farthest corner of the room. The broom was still in his hand and Nil resigned himself to his fate and his lowly status. He had decided to be happy for whoever would be adopted.

The children were getting in their last few moments of practice. Each child was doing, to the best of his ability, the talent or skill that he did best. Some were standing in the line counting, "1…2…3…4…5…" and so on. Others, refusing to be outdone, counted at the top of their voices, "10…20…30…40…50…!" While some turned cartwheels, some hopped on one foot. Some sang their favorite song and others stood around trying to look taller. Still others they flexed their muscles. One little guy stood very still and frown his face up into a scowl as he tried his best to look as if he was thinking deep and very serious thoughts! Another little boy, who was convinced that his smile was his greatest feature, was looking ridiculous as he stretched his mouth with the forefingers of both hands in a vain attempt to smile bigger.

But, Nil just stood in his corner leaning on the handle of the broom. No longer as dejected as he was in the beginning, he found the antics of the other boys funny to watch. He almost felt like he was watching the television. He grinned at the smiley boy and actually chuckled at a little kid who was practicing looking sad so the adoptive parents would feel sorry for him.

Nil couldn't help wondering what kind of people were coming. In his own way and in his own words, Nil asked himself, "Would they be people who would be impressed by all this craziness? Would they pick a boy because he could jump the highest, run the fastest or who was the smartest? Or would they just want a boy who would just want to be their son?"

All of a sudden, Nil's heart leaped! From where he stood he had an unrestricted view of the door. In the doorway stood the most handsome man and the grandest, most beautiful lady Nil had ever seen. The man stood there in a long gray coat with his gray top hat in one hand and a black cane with a gold handle in the other. His black shoes shone like the water that filled the low spot in the back yard after a heavy rain. His face, with dark brown eyes and a mouth that seem to promise a smile at any moment, was the kindest that Nil had ever seen. To Nil, the man's walnut skin gave him the look of father and friend and *home*.

The lady was the woman of Nil's dreams from the feathered hat on her silky auburn hair that cascaded over her shoulders, to the wonderful fur coat, high heel shoes and white gloves. As she stood in the doorway with one white gloved hand holding her husband's strong arm and the other placed on her chest, she was the picture of loveliness. Her hazel eyes were first shocked and then slowly filled with a knowing and a sense of purpose. Those eyes were more beautiful than Nil ever dreamed eyes could be. Even if he never saw these people again, Nil knew he would take this sight of them to his grave. He would never forget this moment for as long as he lived!

In a moment, gone were the thoughts of resignation. Nil knew it would never happen to him *but he wanted it! He wanted this family to adopt him!* He knew they never would, but he would forever see this mother and father when he dreamed in his dreaming place in the attic. They would at the very least make his dreams more real.

Very quickly, the sound in the room died down to nothing as each boy was mesmerized by the grand sight of this grand couple. Recovering from his own awe, the Dorm Master rushed over to the couple, fawning and apologizing for the chaos. He shook the man's hand and drew them into the middle of the room. The boys suddenly remembered their game plan. And they again began to put their talents and skills on display. The noise was almost deafening! Boys were all over the room doing everything but swinging on the chandelier. They sang, danced, cartwheeled, recited the ABC's and even smiled a stretched mouth smile. It was a madhouse!

Only their determination to bring a child home kept the father and mother from making as dignified an exit as possible!

As the woman's eyes looked slowly around the room, they fastened on a little boy who stood in the darkest corner of the room. He was wearing a red and white striped tee shirt under a pair of dirty coveralls that had a button missing so one strap dangled. Here was a little boy whose feet were bare and scarred from many splinters and cuts; a little boy with a dirty face and uncombed hair, and he was leaning on a broom.

Nil was standing with his head down when, little by little, he looked up and saw her look over at him. Very quickly he bowed his little head! He was suddenly very ashamed to be in the presence of these wonderful people looking as he did. He was almost afraid to move, less he draw more attention to himself! He felt the cold hard wall behind him as he shrank as far back into the corner as he could. The *cold* and the *hard* seemed to give him comfort as if they were familiar friends. For *cold and hard* were all that he had known all of his young life.

The grand lady felt her tender heart melt within her. Suddenly, she was oblivious to everyone else in the room. It was as if time had stopped! When later, she thought back on this moment, she would never recall the walk over to the little boy. She would never remember how long it took or how many steps. She would never remember how her high heels clicked their way across the hardwood floor. All she would remember would be the way he looked standing there. Alone in the world; *all alone against the world*! He looked to be so vulnerable yet so durable; so weak but with a resilience that had thus far kept him going; that had not let him truly quit on life. He appeared so empty and yet so filled with potentials and possibilities. He seemed to be filled with the promise of love and the assurance of hope! He seemed to scream tacitly, "Take me home with you! You are my mother and father *and I am your son!*

Nil sensed rather than heard her coming in his direction. Surely she wouldn't approach him! There were too many boys between them. She would certainly stop before she reached him! The boys in the room stopped all of their antics one by one. As she passed each of them, they realized their chance was gone, their window of opportunity had closed! So they stopped to see whom she would choose.

By this time, Nil could hear the clicking of her heels on the hardwood floor. They were getting louder which meant *they were getting closer to him!* Then, the clicking stopped! Nil suddenly caught the scent of the most glorious fragrance he had ever experienced in his life. He was unable to move! The perfume wafted through the air as she took one of her white gloves off. He felt the gossamer touch of an angel when she placed her hand on his head. She was totally unmindful that his hair was uncombed. As she caressed Nil's curly hair, it was as if every movement of her soft hand pulled a tear that had been waiting behind his eyes all of his life to spill over at that moment. And spill over they did! Nil wept soundlessly. He cried unashamedly and fully. He flushed all of the sorrow for his ignoble birth away and all of the sorrow for pains afflicted by every bully of his life. For every biscuit he had to steal and hide. For every time he doubted that this dream would come true and for every kick and slap, he cried. For every stomp and curse that he had endured at the hands of the Dorm Master, he wept.

She looked back at her husband and motion to him with a smile and a nod of her regal head. When he got near enough to hear her, she whispered, "Those other boys want to live in our house – this boy *wants to be part of our home.* They want to leave this place. *He wants to be our son!* The others want to be blessed *and this boy wants to be a blessing.*

The man looked at the boy and indeed he saw a brother for his son and a son for himself. He reached down and, putting his fingers under Nil's chin, he lifted his face so he could see Nil's eyes. Nil did not resist this gentle gesture. He allowed his face to be raised. It was then that he saw the hand of the woman. Wonder of wonders! The ring on her finger was the ring of his dreams. Oh! How the colors *did dance in the light!*

The man spoke to Nil in a voice that was warm and soft, "What is your name, Son?"

"N…, Ni…Nil," said the boy in a sobbing whisper. The man looked over to the Dorm Master and asked, "What is this boy's name?"

"Nil, sir," answered the Dorm Master.

"Do you mean, "Nil," as in *nothing, empty, zero, nonentity?*" the man queried.

"Yes, sir," replied the Dorm Master. One day I found him on the steps of our orphanage. He just never was much more than *nil* in the way that he came here and he was not much of anything in what he did so that's what I always called him. It was just a little joke, Sir."

The man and woman looked at one another and wondered how anyone could be so callused and insensitive as to name a child, "*Nothing.*"

Then the woman did the most amazing thing. She knelt down on the hardwood floor in front of Nil. Taking the broom from his hand and laying it against the wall in the corner, she looked into his face. She saw past the dirty streaks of briny tears; the tears that showed no signs of letting up. She looked until she saw the depth and quality of the love that filled his heart. She looked until she saw more love in those tear-filled eyes than she ever knew a person could hold in his heart. The remarkable thing to her was that despite the fact that she knew that this little boy's heart had been broken all of his young life, she could see that not one drop of the purest love a child had ever been blessed to have had leaked out!

And then, to Nil's greatest surprise, she pulled him to her and buried his head in the soft, heavenly scented folds of her fur coat! It was then that Nil thought he was most assuredly dreaming! He heard the words of an angel and felt the caress of her love as she breathed the eleven most beautiful words that had ever been spoken to him, "Will you please come home with us and be our son?"

Nil looked full into her face and could scarcely believe his eyes! This grandest of all ladies was crying, and for him! He felt the large drops of her tears fall on his feet. Then he remembered his dirty, scarred feet! He wanted to hide them but there was nowhere to put them. Sensing his embarrassment, she looked down and took her pristine white gloves and tenderly began to wipe his feet dry of her tears.

It was then that Nil felt another set of arms around his and this angel in a fur coat! The man was kneeling with them and he was holding them both. And to Nil's surprise, he was softly, gently weeping as only the strongest of men can. His voice was low and husky with joy as he promised, "Son, if you will come home with us and complete our family, we will live the rest of our lives to make you happy and keep you safe!"

The Dorm Master picked that time to rush over and exclaimed, "You don't want him! He is only Nil! He isn't the strongest or the smartest. He isn't good enough for you! Look around again!" the Dorm Master said with his hands sweeping in a wide arc around the room.

The man stood up and seemed to Nil to stand taller than when he first entered the room. "Yes! We do want him if he will have us! And as long as we are together as a family we will be as strong as we need to be. Furthermore, we are smart! And we will not allow ignorance and small mindedness to cheat us out of our son and our first son's brother.

Nil looked around the room at all of the bullies. He saw all of the boys who had no mother and father and he pitied them. He looked at the Dorm Master and thought that maybe he pitied him the most. Somehow, Nil knew that the Dorm Master would never be as happy as Nil was right then.

He looked at the dining room that he had eaten his last meal in. And he looked back at the Dorm Master who would punish him no more! Nil threw his shoulders back and lifted his head and with his new father holding one hand and the grandest lady in the world (his new mother) holding his other hand. With them, Nil walked out of that building forever.

Nil's mouth dropped open and his hands flew up to cover both sides of his face when they stepped out of the large double doors of the orphanage. At the curb, the only car in sight was a long white stretch limousine! The driver was standing tall in a black uniform at the back door of the automobile waiting for them. He held the door open and they all stepped into the limousine and entered the world of Nil's dreams.

Chapter 24

From "Nil" to "Noble"

There are many people who feel that they are born by happenstance; that their birth was more accepted than planned and desired. This disconnect with Divine Purpose leaves that hurting heart vulnerable to negativities that are simply a part of life. There seems to be as many, if not more, things in life that are designed to break one down than the number of things that are here to build one up! There are people, Watchers, that God places in our lives whose purpose is to build us up so that we will feel the self-worth that causes us to persevere, never quit and win just because we feel that we deserve the victory; we deserve to be champions!

It was late that night. His new brother, Junior, was sound asleep in the lower bunk. Nil lay awake with his eyelids closed trying to see all over again everything that had happened that day. He didn't bother trying to put the events in chronological order. He just remembered things as they were triggered in his mind by other thoughts. He remembered looking through the moon roof of the limo and seeing the Dorm Master and all of the guys on the steps and at the windows watching him leave.

Nil recalled the face of one little fellow in particular who was bullied almost as badly as he had been. He saw the little guy's face peering out of the big bay window in the library. Nil felt sorry for the little guy because he knew the misery that was ahead for him. But mostly, he felt sorry for him because he knew the boy didn't know how to pretend. Pretending was Nil's escape from the world that was his nightmare to the world of his dreams.

One day, Nil had told this kid about his dream family and the little guy just couldn't see any sense to it. He didn't say anything against it – he just said, "Let's go to the swings." Nil now believed that his new life happened *because he dreamed it hard enough!*

In his mind's eye, Nil saw again the boulevard that the limo had cruised down going to his new house. The large trees that lined the street and the beautiful houses with their impeccably manicured lawns would be indelibly printed in Nil's mind. He knew that the homes that they passed were the grandest he had ever seen. But when the boulevard ended in a cul-de-sac that turned into a wide concrete driveway and that driveway winded around beautiful stately Oak trees and Crepe Myrtles toward a huge white mansion, he felt that he had entered into heaven.

While he reflected on the events of the day, Nil absentmindedly chewed on one of the two rolls that he had sneaked from the dinner table. He had never had this kind of bread before. As he munched, the reality continued to sink in that he didn't live at the orphanage anymore. Nil knew beyond any shadow of doubt that dreams really do come true!

On the first evening, as Nil and his new family were eating dinner, his father taught him the meaning of the word, "nil." Nil decided immediately that he wanted to change it. So, one of the first major changes he wanted to make in his new life was to change his name.

Nil thought long and hard about this. He thought about what he wanted people to think about when they called his name. He knew the kind of person he wanted to be. He wanted to be a good and respectable, honorable and trustworthy person. His mother heard him describe the kind of person he wanted to be.

"Why, Son, those are such noble desires. As a matter of fact, I would truly like to call you 'Noble'." The way his new mother pronounced "Noble" sounded so grand and powerful that he decided he would forever be, "Noble".

A few days later, Noble was laying on his bunk trying to take in all of the events that had changed his life. He knew that he would never be the same again. He realized that for the first time in a very long time he hadn't needed to dream his favorite dream. "'Cause I'm too busy living it." Noble said to himself. He was the son of the grandest lady and the most wonderful father. He thought about the dream that had been his greatest treasure. He also remembered the book he had read about the rich family who lived in a mansion. Noble thought about something that was still missing. In the book the family dressed up and went to the opera. Noble had never been to one but had seen pictures of operas in books. He was interested in the opera because it had the combined features of being live and on stage but it also brought fantasies to life. Thus, he had always wanted to see one.

One morning at the breakfast table, Noble asked, "Mom, have you ever seen an opera?"

"Why yes, Noble," she answered in surprise, "Why do you ask?" Noble made a big show of just stirring his Grits. "I- I just wondered is all."

"Would you like to go the opera? We have season tickets."

"Yes, Maam. I would like to go someday."

The very next Saturday found Noble and his family in their stretch limo on their way to see an opera. The parents were seated with their faces forward while their sons, Noble and Junior, were seated facing them, play a video game.

Their father, dressed in black tuxedo, was trying to get a quick nap on the way. He called it a "Power Nap." Their beautiful mother was dressed in an evening gown that Noble thought must have been borrowed from an angel. It was a very light pink with gossamer lace around the shoulders. Her pearl necklace was an exquisite match for her diamond and pearl earrings. As the boys played and teased one another their mother simply glowed with love, pride and thanksgiving for them.

As she watched them she tried to imagine the hardships that had been in Noble's life from birth. These thoughts reminded her that the maid had informed her that she had been finding bread crumbs, wilted pieces of celery and carrots and even some smushed grapes in Noble's pants pockets. For a few days this had been a mystery to them all. Gradually, they began to understand that in the orphanage, Noble must have acquired the habit of sneaking things from the dinner table to eat later.

The wise mother also noticed that Noble was having a difficult time adjusting to his new privilege and status of son and brother. As the adoption was still so new, this gentlewoman was not stressed about these things. However, she decided to take more clearly defined steps to help Noble enter his new life with a feeling of belonging.

In her reverie, the loving mother had turned away from the boys and was staring out the car window at nothing that the physical eyes could see. Slowly, she turned her attention back to the interior of the car and noted that her husband had finally surrendered to a much need nap. The game was over and Junior was reading one of his comic books that he kept stashed everywhere he knew he would spend time.

She looked at Noble at the same time that he looked at her. Their eyes met. Noble grinned shyly as his mother motioned him to come and sit by her. Noble was still quite taken with the grandeur and loveliness of this most gracious lady. He still had not come to an acceptable reason for this wonderful family adopting him.

She moved over to make room for him. In her soft and totally disarming voice that spoke with an intimacy that is patently a mother's way and privilege, she asked, Noble, do you realize how very much we all love you and need you in our lives?"

For some reason it was hard for Noble to look at her as he shook his curly head, "No."

"Son, when Junior was born, we were the happiest parents we knew. We were full of love for him and gratitude to God for His wonderful gift. But, Noble, we didn't choose Junior. We couldn't choose Junior! We could only accept him or reject him. But when we went to that terrible orphanage, we could have picked any boy there. We could have picked a taller boy or a shorter one, an older boy or a younger boy. We could have picked one with a lighter complexion or a darker one; a smarter boy or one less intelligent. But we chose you! We decide *we wanted you!* We didn't just want any boy. We wanted the boy who would be so special that he could fit into our family and be *our son* – not just *our boy*! We wanted you! When your name was "Nil" which means *nothing, zero, nobody* - we wanted you! Before you had done anything that would make us proud of you (which I am sure you will) – we wanted you! When we saw you, Son, it was as if you outshined every other little boy there. After we saw you the other boys didn't have a chance!"

When his mother first started talking, the things she said made Noble smile. But as she kept talking and he began to get a glimpse of her heart, Noble got so glad that his smiling eyes begin to fill up with tears.

His mother could tell that he was crying. She also knew that the tears were of joy and thanksgiving. She turned his face up to his so she could look straight into his eyes.

"Do you understand now, Noble, how important you are to your new family?" she asked. Noble nodded his head up and down and snuggled up to her.

They had not known it but while his mother was talking, Junior had closed his comic book and was listening and enjoying every word he heard. Through his tears Noble looked over at his brother. His joy got even fuller when through his tears he saw his brother give him what looked like a blurry thumbs up. He wiped his eyes and clearly saw Junior. And he really was giving him a two handed thumbs up!

That night the opera was all that Noble had thought it would be and more!

CHAPTER 25

WE WANTED ANOTHER
SON – WE GOT A BOY

There is no shortage of Christians who have not learned whom God says they are! Then, there are those who have just enough faith in God to know that they are saved from their sins but not enough faith to believe that they are "save to new life sublime," (as the song says). Still others feel so unworthy to be true sons of God that they just can't see themselves as blessed as others in the church seem to be. These are envious of other's testimonies; they never feel that they are as spiritual as others appear to be. They never imagine that God can use them to do any great thing. They praise God for the testimonies of others but secretly harbor resentfulness against those they deem to be favored over themselves. And what of those who can't believe that their relationship with God is all that the Bible says it is!

In a similar way Noble just is not able to assimilate into his adoptive family. They are doing everything they can think of doing to make it easy for Noble to be family but he just doesn't get it!

It was the day after graduation. The family was sitting at the table in the dining room. The dinner was perfect as usual and the servants had cleared the table. Normally, the family would have retired to the family room but this time they just stayed at the table to finish their discussion.

The boys were eighteen years old. Noble almost never sneaked bread and cookies from the table but when he did, it was because he was stressed or otherwise bothered. For some reason that he could not name, he had never come to the place where he really felt that he was a son of his adoptive father and mother in the same way that Junior was their son.

The parents never loved either son more than the other. What they did for one - they did for the other. One would never know from the way they were treated that both were not the biological sons of their parents. Despite all the things they did that should have demonstrated to Noble that he was truly their son, Noble never felt it in his heart. When he wanted something that he thought was very costly, he felt that he wasn't worthy of it. Often, he just didn't mention it. At other times Noble would begin his request with a report of the newest things Junior had been given. Frequently, he tried to do something that was very special in order to cause his parents to feel that they owed him. His parents tried in every way they knew to make Noble understand that they wanted to give to him just because *he was their son and they loved him!*

In every social setting, Noble was able to fit properly *except at home.* As some people never lose their accent when speaking a new language, Noble never quite managed to adjust into his role of son. When he was tired or was preoccupied with thoughts, he still found himself snatching his foot back sometimes when he talked to his father. And though there was never any reason for this behavior, he still recoiled at times when someone came upon him suddenly. It was more than that he was startled. He actually expected to be hit with something or kicked.

The boys were smart in school. Their grades were good enough for them to go to any university of their choice. Junior was, by his nature, competitive, and Noble developed the will to win from Junior. They both excelled academically and athletically.

Having been out of town on business for the company he owned and served as CEO, the father was taking this opportunity to discuss with his sons the gift that he and their mother would give them for a graduation present. He also wanted to know what university they wanted to attend.

"Noble, what would you like to receive for your graduation present?"

Noble had been thinking about this question for quite a while. He didn't want to ask for more than he could reasonably expect to receive because he couldn't stand rejection and being denied.

"Dad, Mom, I really appreciate all of that you have done for me. You didn't know this but about a month ago I got a flat on the rear tire of my bicycle. If you can see your way to fixing it, I could ride my bike to the Junior College where I want to go to school."

"Is that all?" his parents exclaimed disappointedly. "Are you sure this is what you want?"

"Yes! That is all I want," Noble replied.

The parents turned to Junior. "And what gift would you like, Junior?" his mother asked.

"I would appreciate a brand new bright red Ferrari sports car. I would look real cool driving around the campus of Harvard University. That's where I want to go to school!"

After their young graduates had left the room the loving parents looked at one another and wondered at what they had just witnessed. They had loved both of their sons. They knew they agreed with the choices Junior made but were disappointed and appalled at Noble's.

Noble's mother sat back in her chair with her graceful hands in her lap. Her beautiful auburn hair had little wisps of silver around the edges of her temple as if the gentle angels of time had softly caressed her. Her matched pearl earrings were perfect compliments to her pearl necklace. She was the picture of grace and poise; aristocracy and strength; love and compassion. "We should have expected something like this," the mother whispered in a voice that was mellow and filled with concern. "Noble never was able to ask for the best thing."

Noble's father sat at the table with his head in his hands. He seemed to have aged visibly. Gone was the confident air of one who is in control; gone was the ramrod straight posture of one who is in authority. His shoulders were slumped in a posture of defeat. His hands were sweating and clammy. And those usually alert and piercing eyes were blinded by the briny tears that even now were flowing in tiny rivulets down his mahogany cheeks. His wife looked at him and that sight threatened to break her heart. She had never seen him stripped of him strength. He was always so able; so capable! To see him totally acquiescent was more than she could bear.

She heard a sound that came from deeper than his chest. It had its origin in the primal depths of the deepest echelon of his humanity. The groan defied defining and yet would be universally understood by all who have failed in their greatest endeavor of life. This sound of grief would be understood with copious clarity by all who have ever known the agony of the conquered. For, try as he might, he knew finally and completely that Noble would never be his son in the pure sense of the word.

Even in his anguish, his analytical mind took over. He realized that Noble's adoption was pure and real to his wife, their son, Junior and himself. But Noble would always see himself through the eyes of an orphan; a stepchild; a foster child. This grieving father knew beyond any shadow of doubt that the elements necessary for Noble to step into the reality of son ship was infinitely more than man's law could provide.

"I didn't merely want another boy to raise, Honey, *I wanted another son!*" I thought that we could make him our son. But I know now that I can only make myself his father and you can only make yourself his mother. *Only he can make himself our son*! He being our son has less to do with him seeing us as parents than it does him seeing himself as our son. If he is, *in his heart,* our son, it will naturally follow that he will behave as our son!"

"Yes, Dear," the gentle mother answered. I know that you are right but let's not give up on him. Who knows what our challenges would be today if we had started out in life as he did."

CHAPTER 26

I AM MY FATHER'S SON – MY BROTHER IS NOT!

Who can teach a boy how to be a son? Where can a son spirit be purchased? What is the formula that when mixed with water produces, in the heart of a boy – a son?

Junior realized, finally, that Noble is never going to become his brother and his parent's son! He is hurting in ways that he never knew he could! You see, dear reader, sometimes the Watcher cannot succeed! NO Watcher can effect positive change in the life of one who will not change! Though the Watched one may desire to change, if he doesn't change, no matter the sleeping place reason – THE WATCHER FAILS IN HIS MISSION!

As was his way when he had something on his mind that defied his understanding, Junior went down to the stable and saddled Chico, his beautiful Palomino gelding. Chico stood a full sixteen hands tall. He was dark gold in color with a light blond mane and tail. His blond forelock was thick and so long that it hung down past his eyes.

After checking the fit of the saddle and bridle, Junior stepped into the stirrup and swung himself up on the horse. For a moment he felt Chico tremble in anticipation. The Palomino pranced and danced and tossed his head as if to say, "What are you waiting for? Let me go *now!*" The young man felt the same excitement and though it wasn't necessary, he spurred the great horse and felt the adrenaline rush as Chico gathered his muscles and flung himself into full a gallop. The rider felt the familiar sensation of flying. The horse might have been the mythological Pegasus as they sped across the back pasture toward the lake. He seemed not to touch the ground as he headed past the paddock where the mares in foal were grazing. He was going to his "Thinking Tree." The wind ran its breathy fingers threw Junior's short wavy hair and toyed gently with the sleeves of his shirt. Chico's long thick mane whipped across the young man's face with such force that the stinging added to the thrill of the ride. Junior could feel the power of the gelding as the horse reached for each yard of turf in ever widening strides. The powerful hindquarters were thrusting forward harder and harder and the strong forelegs were pulling faster and ever faster. His spurs were not needed. Neither was the short quirt that was held tightly in Junior's right hand.

In the moonlit night, the soft staccato beat of Chico's hooves was only faintly heard being muffled by the thick short grass. Junior thought to spur the speeding equine as they approached the hill where the lake rested on top. But he knew that Chico couldn't give any more than he was giving. Taking the hill in great strides, Chico barely slowed but never faltered. Junior reached the hill's summit and reined the great horse in just at the edge of the water. He stopped so suddenly that Chico reared up and fought the air with his front feet flailing. His shod hooves flashed in the moonlight. All Chico was trying to show was that he still had much speed and power left in reserve. Chico still wanted to run! He fought the bit but couldn't win. Finally, he just stood there beautiful and proud and he was only slightly winded. Junior dismounted and tethered his gelding to the old Oak tree that had stood watch over the lake long before Junior discovered it. Chico soon got the idea that his master wanted him to be still. Chico quieted himself except that he occasionally pawed the ground.

The form fitting shroud that was the night softly covered everything with a silvery iridescence. Junior stood under the leafy canopy of the Oak tree. He began to drink in the nocturnal tranquility. The silhouette of the young man was still as he stood on the grassy knoll at the water's edge. Standing under the old Oak tree next to his horse, Junior appeared frozen for the moment with one hand resting in the crotch of the tree and the other absentmindedly tangling his fingers in the mane of his horse.

"What's wrong with Noble? Why can't he just see that he is our father's son just as I am?" Junior exploded. The sudden sound startled the horse. The gelding threw his head up and sidled away from the young man.

Moving out from under the tree and to the water's edge, the young man, in anger and frustration picked up a flat rock and hurled it across the water in an amazing seven pointer. He was momentarily diverted by the seven pointer. After all these years of skipping rocks on water he still got a sense of accomplishment and a rush of victory from making a rock skip seven or more times. As Junior stood on the bank he watched the ripples from the sinking rock approach him. Somehow, watching the ripples come home to the bank where they always end up brought the sorrowful young man back to the issue at hand.

"Noble, why can't you just be our father's son and my brother?" Junior soliloquized. "What more can be said or done to make you know that we see you as family in the same sense that we all are family? Our father and mother are willing to give you anything that their money and position can afford!" Junior knew that Noble was nowhere around but these were things that he had said to Noble for years and the familiar words just tumbled forth. Despite all the many things that Junior had ever said to Noble about being family – *he just didn't seem to get it!*

Chico snorted and pawed the ground impatiently. Junior was shaken back to the day's realities. While he was thinking of today's events, he remembered times when Noble asked their father for things Junior knew their father wouldn't (*no couldn't*) give him. Like the time he wanted his father to buy him a shotgun because Noble's friend, Rodney has a B.B. gun and Noble, for some reason, always wanted to have something that was better or bigger than his friends. Junior had expected his father to say "No!" And true to form, his father said "No!" There was just no way that their wise and loving father could give Noble a shotgun. Noble hadn't understood and even had muttered under his breath, "You would have said *'Yes'* to Junior!" Junior had heard him but had never told anyone.

He remembered when had even tried to share with Noble an experience he'd had just after his eighth birthday. He saw it in his mind just as if it had happened yesterday.

Before Jenkins, the chauffeur, could open the door, Junior had opened it himself, jumped out of the car and ran into the house.

"Dad, Dad!" He'd called. "Where are you?" He remembered running through the foyer and through the living room. "Dad!" Junior ran down the hall past the library to his father's office. He burst through the door. "Dad!"

His father had looked up from his desk where he was working with his computer. "Hi, Junior, what's going on?"

He was accustomed to Junior being excited. He was always on an adventure. A passionate child by nature, Junior was usually in high gear. When he was happy – he was ecstatic. When he was sad – he was terribly despondent.

"Dad, Dad," Junior gasped, out of breath.

"Slow down, Son," his father instructed. "Take a deep breath and tell me what's on your mind."

"Dad, Johnny Jamison told me that his father almost never gives him what he asks for! He said his father always tells him things costs too much or Johnny doesn't need it or he's too young to have it! Then he asked me if you, Dad, ever give me anything I want."

"What did you tell him, Junior?"

"I told him that you almost always give me what I ask for!"

"Junior, why do you think I give you so much of what you ask for?"

Junior replied, "That's easy Dad, 'cause you love me so much! I mean, you gave me my own computer, a brand new

Play Station, a big screen TV in my bedroom and more toys than I will ever wear out. And what about last year when you and Mom had planned that we would all go to Paris for the summer. When you knew that I wanted to go to Disney World, Magic Kingdom, Epcot Center in Orlando Florida and even Disney Land and Universal Studios in California, you changed all your plans and took me where I wanted to go. I never even found out about the sacrifice until last month. You didn't have to do all of that.

"His father nodded and smiled. "Yes, Junior, I do love you. But, there are things that I do for you because I have to *whether I love you or not* and *whether I want to or not, that is, unless I don't mind going to jail.* I provide a roof over your head, food for your stomach, medical help when you get sick and an education. I do love you very much but *I do these things because I am your father.*" Being your father is a thing of blood and there is nothing that we can do to change that. I can only accept or reject that but we are all stuck with its reality. That you have my nose and your mother's eyes, your mother's smile and my hair are truths we must deal with. However, there are things I do for you – not because I am your father but *because you are my son!* "You see, Junior, for you to be my son has less to do with me and more to do with you."

Junior looked quizzically at his father and declared, "I don't understand that, Dad. How can I have anything to do with being your son? I thought I was born your son. Are you saying *I was adopted?*"

Pushing himself back from his desk, the loving father looked full into his son's face. "Junior, when you were born I was your father. I didn't adopt you. But in a way we can say

156

that as you grew up *you adopted me.* As you grew up, without you realizing it *you studied me!* You learned me. You know the kinds of decisions I make. You know the kinds things I will approve for you. So, when you ask me for things, you ask a son who knows his father. You rarely request things that I won't or can't approve."

"Oh, now I get it! Maybe Johnny just doesn't know his dad the way I know my father!" Junior was grinning from ear to ear.

Junior walked over to his Dad and looked up at him. Something passed from one to the other; an intimacy that only true fathers and sons share.

In his mind's eye, Junior saw himself hug his father and say, "I am so glad that *I am my father's son!*"

CHAPTER 27

I DON'T WANT TO GO BUT
I JUST CAN'T STAY!

There are some whose thoughts center on the things they don't have more than the things they have. My son, Lamar says, "Where the focus goes – the power flows!" In order words, what you focus on you will build on!

Noble cannot go after what is not there because he is so obsessed with what he perceives is there! It's like he is giving a war but nobody is coming but I am my Father's son – my Brother is coming but himself! If he refuses to be instructed by his Watchers, he is relegated to the ends that he provides for himself! Noble left the dinner table and went up to his bedroom. In all the world this was the place that he loved best. Always, in the orphanage, he had shared has sleeping place with twenty or more boys. Always he wished he had a bedroom of his own, So, when Noble and Junior finally grew to where each wanted to explore his individuality the wise parents gave Noble his own room.

He flopped on the bed face down. With his head in his hands, he whispered fiercely into the bedspread, "What's wrong with me? I know Dad and Mom wanted to give me something much better than a bicycle repair! Why am I always so afraid that if I ask for too much I'll become a burden on them? I know they love me!" he reasoned. "Why can't I be like Junior?"

He wasn't jealous of Junior; he just wanted to be a part of the family with a kind of reckless abandon. He didn't want to always feel that he had to somehow "measure up" or "fit in."

Noble remembered the look of disappointment that passed between his parents when he told them his desire. Then, when Junior had requested the same things Noble had really wanted for himself, Noble realized that he would never belong in this wonderful family.

The problem was that he knew that they all really loved him. His mother, the most beautiful, gracious and tender heart in the world; his father, the kindest and most loving man Noble had ever met, and Junior his devoted brother – loved him more than life itself. "Maybe that is the problem," Noble wondered. "Maybe I just don't deserve that kind of love! "I can't stay here any longer where I don't belong! I will always be grateful to them for getting me out of the orphanage but I now know that I cannot stay in this wonderful family under false pretenses."

Noble didn't know how to break the news to them but he would not be cowardly and sneak off without talking to them. He felt that it would be easier to tell Junior, so got up from the bed and put his riding boots on. He thought that Junior was probably down by the pond.

He went out the side door because it was nearest to the stables. As he walked around the house, he tried not to think of what he wanted to say because he didn't want to sound rehearsed. The gravel crunched beneath his feet as he walked up the path. The stable was empty and darkening with just a little light coming in through the large doors that were at each end of the stable. His beautiful black and white mare, Shadow Dancer, caught his scent and nickered softly. Her perfectly formed head stuck out over the bottom half of the stall door.

Noble went to the tack room and picked out her saddle and bridle. She took the bit readily, anticipating the outing. Stepping into the saddle, Noble could not see the worry lines on his forehead. But, he was worried. This was the most important decision he had ever made.

He was glad for the momentary distraction that Shadow Dancer provided him as she danced and prance as she strained at the bit trying to move out.

"Easy, Shadow, easy girl," Noble softly said. He walked her the first one hundred yards. Then he loosened his hold on the reins and let some slip free, giving her some rein. Shadow Dancer broke into a slow canter. She was glad for the canter but tossed her head and tried to get more rein so she could run free. Noble continued to hold her in.

He was fighting against his own feelings. He didn't want to leave this family. *He just felt that he couldn't stay!*

Looking ahead, Noble saw the hill. Beyond it was the pond. Shadow Dancer settled down and accepted that she couldn't run any faster. If his mind had not been so preoccupied with the business at hand, Noble would have enjoyed the ride. The wind was playing tag with Shadow Dancer's mane and tail. The breeze felt cool and comforting on Noble's face.

The moon was just coming out and the overcast sky was letting the moonglow shine in intermittent lighting. The forecasters had promised rain showers with the possibility of stormy weather. But as of now, the weather was perfect for a night ride. Coming up over the top of the hill, Noble saw Junior at the water's edge.

Chapter 28

From "Noble" Back to "Nil"

Oft times, trying to be is counter-productive when all that one has to do is simply - be! If it's raining outside, one doesn't have to salt the clouds, do a rain dance or even pray for rain! It's raining outside! Just get out there in it if you want to get wet!

Noble is less about being a success and more about figuring out the process! He can imagine all kinds of reasons for not being a son and a brother! He just cannot accept that he already is what he is struggling to become! He is like a fellow who is sitting down and looking for a chair to sit on! What Watcher can help him?

The sound of muffled hooves broke the stillness. It was not that the sound was so loud that Junior had to hear it. Rather, it was the incongruence of the sound in comparison to the sound of the crickets chirping, the songs of the night birds, and the water lapping at the pond's edge. All the sounds seem to play the very natural and beautiful harmony of nature's symphony. Then, the music of the night that easily flows without cadence and tempo was interrupted by the staccato rhythm of a horse's hoof beats. Junior turned to face the sound and knew who it was. Just as he looked toward the sound, he heard his brother's horse, Shadow Dancer, whinny as he picked up the scent of Chico. Chico pawed the ground and whinnied his answer.

In the way that was patently Noble's he rode fast up to his brother, Junior. Reining his horse in, Noble grinned down at his brother. "I knew I would find you here."

"I hoped you would too, Junior answered, "'Cause I want to ask you something."

"What's up?'

"Well, I really don't know just how to word it so you may have to read between the lines to understand what I'm trying to say."

"I'll do my best," Noble promised.

"Noble, I know that I am your brother and you are my brother. And I know that my father and mother are your parents. But what I am not sure of is whether you are their son! You don't seem to think of yourself as their son. Oh, I know you are aware of all the things they are *supposed* to do for you. But you don't seem to understand all of the things they *want* to do for you; things that they don't owe you legally but they will do for you *if you will just be their son.*

"But "Noble started to speak.

"No! Noble, I want you to tell me the truth! *Are you our father's son?*"

"I want to be and there are times that I do feel that I fit in more than at other times."

"But, don't you see, Noble, you don't have *to feel that you fit*! You *do fit us* because *we are molded around you!* You seem to be the only one who doesn't know this!"

163

Junior didn't know just when it had started but he realized that it was raining. Not hard. The rain was just a soft misting spray. It was just moist enough that the soft summer wind cooled him off. He was enjoying the refreshing moment when he looked up and saw the ominous clouds.

"Noble, we'd better finish this talk later! Let's get back before those clouds let go!" Junior gathered Chico's reins and stepped into the saddle. Both young men clicked to their horses and moved out at a slow canter. They were surprised when the wind picked up and they could hear the heavy raindrops fall closer and closer. Suddenly, they felt the stinging, pelting rain on the back of their necks. As if that wasn't bad enough, they heard the crack of hailstones smacking trees and rocks! When the first hailstone about the size of a lemon hit Shadow Dancer, he leaped into a full run. Chico picked up on Shadow Dancer's fear and ignored Junior who was sawing at the reins to slow him down and regain control. Chico, with nostrils flaring and his ears laid back, stretched out and ran low to the ground. He and Shadow Dancer ran neck and neck. Neither was racing the other. Both were finding comfort in matching the other stride for stride as they tried to outdistance a common enemy. They had the same motivation. Get away from the wild night that threatened to kill them. The hailstones were no longer stinging – they were causing real pain! Not only were the hailstones pummeling the horses, the riders were taking a beating as well! The large hailstones were hitting with such force and regularity that they were finally taking their toll on the bodies of the two young men. Junior's right eye was swollen almost completely shut. And Noble was fighting to stay conscious from the constant beating.

The hailstones were falling furiously, as if to satisfy a vendetta against the two brothers. Running on open grazing land, they had nothing to take shelter under. The wind driven rain was coming down in torrents. No longer were they dealing with raindrops! The brothers were trying to survive a wall of water that produced pin pricks on their exposed skin. The rain sliced at them from a sharp angle as the wind blew into their faces. Hailstones seemed to be bigger than when they started out. The night lit up in flashes of lightening streaks. These light displays were accompanied by the peal and ever heightening repeal of thunder. The crashes and explosions of thunder and the flashes of lightening completed the chaos of a world gone mad!

The horses were almost completely out of their rider's control. Their instincts drove them back to the stable and to their stalls. Gone was the obedience that they were bred and trained to give. Gone was their trust in their masters. They were mindless bodies of powerful motion and fear-crazed horseflesh. As they ran at breakneck speed down the hill toward the stable which was now in easy view, Shadow Dancer lost his footing. Suddenly, he tumbled head over heels! Noble was thrown from the saddle and landed on his back. Chico was a little to the rear and the left of Shadow Dancer, so Junior saw the fall. Junior saw Shadow Dancer go down but then he saw her getting up. She must have been all right because she ran toward the safety of the stable and her warm dry stall.

Unable to stop Chico by pulling on the reins with one hand on each rein, Junior grabbed the left rein with both hands. He pulled back so hard that Chico's head was dragged around to the left - slowing the horse. Chico slowed down enough so that Junior could jump from the saddle. Then Chico ran off behind Shadow Dancer toward his stall.

Junior ran back to where Noble lay. Noble was groaning and writhing in pain. Blood was trickling out of his mouth and his right leg was at an unnatural angle. "Noble!" Junior cried. "Noble! Can you hear me?"

Noble knew that he was badly hurt. He felt himself getting cold, colder than the night. From somewhere in his mind the irony of it all hit him. He was planning to somehow tell Junior that he was leaving but he really did mean to go as far as he knew he now had to go. He heard Junior call his name. "Noble, open your eyes!" Junior commanded. Noble groaned and opened his eyes.

"Junior," he whispered. "Look in my pocket. Is my biscuit still there?"

Junior could hear air bubbles in Noble's voice as he spoke each word. "W-what did you say, Noble?"

Noble struggled to get the words out. "Look in my p-pocket, the right one and see if my b-biscuit is still there!"

Noble couldn't understand what was going on. But he pushed his hands into Noble's rain soaked pocket and pulled out crumbs of what used to be a biscuit.

"Give it to me, Junior." Junior placed the crumbs in Noble's open hand.

"Thanks, brother. T-t-tell Dad and Mom I said I love them and thanks f-for e-everyth-th…." In the driving rain Junior could not be sure what was happening. Just then the lightning flashed illuminating Noble's face and Junior saw Noble's eyes staring into the storm – *seeing nil!*

CHAPTER 29

"BUDDY AND HER"

The Fence Walker

What are the most essential needs of a twelve-year-old boy? It is really a bicycle or a catcher's mitt? Is it the homerun that wins the game? Or could it sometimes be something that thrills and comforts his heart? God, the consummate Watcher has the answer!

The summer sun was warm and comforting this June morning. The trees sighed contentedly as the soft, easy breeze moved gently over their leaves. The sky was a clear baby blue color with large puffy clouds that could easily be daydreamed into fighter planes, wonderfully brave and terrible fierce Indians, great majestic mountains or just about anything.

The Robin Redbreast that sang it's "Good morning" to the world seemed to brag in its song that this day would certainly be a day worth living!

"Buddy!" my mother called. "Buddy, it's time to get up now! You'll be late for Vacation Bible school!"

I was instantly wide awake! "Vacation Bible School!" I said to myself. "What time is it?" I wondered. I glanced across the room to the clock on my dresser. My mother wouldn't let me keep it on the nightstand next to my bed stand. She had to leave for work before it was time for me to get up. And when the alarm went off, I always hit the snooze button a few more times and ended up late for school. I saw that it was eight o' clock, an hour before Vacation Bible Starts. An hour before *She would be there!* She was so special to me! And what was this that I felt for her that kept Her on my mind? Her face kept appearing to me whenever I had a quiet moment. Sometimes, it seemed that I saw Her everywhere I looked and at other times, I couldn't dream Her up no matter how hard I tried! At still other times, it seemed that I could even smell Her perfume when the wind blew just right.

I never felt this way about anyone when I was eleven! Was this just something that happened when you were preparing to be a teenager; a thirteen-year-old? If so, I wish that I hadn't taken this long to get to my twelfth birthday!

Now, nobody knew that I couldn't keep my mind off of Her. No one ever dreamed that I knew that She had to be the most beautiful girl in the world; with Her cute little turned up nose that wrinkled up in the cutest way when She frowned. And this was whether She frowned in deep thought or in very dignified and oh, so justified, exasperation and annoyance. Her eyes were so big and round and how they danced when she laughed! I loved Her soft wavy black hair that shined so bright in the summer sun. Her light honey colored skin was just perfect for Her dark brown eyes. She would be there!

Today, I didn't wait to be told to make my bed and sweep my bedroom floor. I didn't want to take any chances that my mother would inspect my work and maybe find something for me to do that would make me late for Vacation Bible school.

I quickly ate my breakfast (being careful not to "crowd my mouth" as my mother called putting too much food in my mouth at one time). And I chewed all my food thoroughly.

"May I be excused from the table?" I asked.

"Yes! But make sure you comb your hair, brush your teeth. And be sure to wash your face and hands again!" She replied.

My mother really didn't need to tell me to make myself presentable. Wasn't *She* going to be there? I combed my hair making sure my part was straight. I hurriedly brushed my teeth and washed my face and hands. This was truly a special day, so I went to my father and mother's room and got some of my father's Old Spice cologne. I poured some on my hands and dabbed it on my face. When I looked in the mirror at myself I had to smile. My hair was combed just right and the Old Spice smelled so good.

I looked down at my "church shoes" that I had polished last night until they shone like black glass. I gazed back into the mirror and squared my shoulders back. She would like everything about me today. No one could have found a wrinkle in my tee shirt for a million dollars and I had ironed the crease in my blue jeans just right!

"I'm gone, Mama!" I cried as I raced down the stairs. I ran across the vacant lot that was between my house and the church. Just as I came to the sidewalk and before I turned in front of the church I looked to my right and – I SAW HER! She was coming up the sidewalk toward the vacant lot. Her path would bring Her directly in front of where I was. I saw Her but She hadn't seen me yet. Actually, it seemed to me that She had never seen me! She had never given me any indication that She had ever noticed me! Even when I chewed my gum and popped it so loud that our Sunday school teacher had made me come up to the front and apologize to the class for the disturbance - She hadn't shown any sign that She saw me! And when I burped so loud and long that all of the children laughed – I still seemed invisible to Her!

Then it hit me! It was a brilliant idea! It would surely make Her notice me! I scampered back across the parking lot and across the alley to the old dilapidated fence that separated Junebug's backyard from the alley. I knew that I was probably the best climber and balancer in the neighborhood. I climbed the old fence and steadied myself. The old fence creaked and groaned as if in a losing fight with age and gravity. It was already leaning but now the old fence was really straining to stay up straight.

I checked to see where She was and sure enough – She had just then reached the parking lot. In the stillness of the early morning, I knew that the sound of my whistling would carry all of the way over to where She was walking. I began to whistle the theme to the Davy Crockett TV program. It really didn't matter what I whistled, *so long as She heard me.* I pretended that I didn't see Her but out of the corner of my eye I saw Her stop and look at me. I moved my hands wildly in the air to make it seem as though I was falling! I saw Her put her hands to Her mouth as if to hold back a scream. Then I saw the admiration in Her big round eyes when I finally steadied myself. She ran over to the fence and looked up at me. "You are so strong and so brave, Buddy!" She exclaimed.

My plan to get her attention was working! My heart felt as if it would melt. I didn't even know that She knew my name. And the way She said, *"Buddy!"* I never thought my name could sound so wonderful! The way She said it made me feel as though I could do anything. She didn't know it but from that moment on my heart *belonged to Her*!

"Have you ever worked in the circus?" She wanted to know.

"No. I haven't worked in a circus, *yet,*" I replied, "But someday I might. 'Cause this is easy if you know what you're doin.'"

I remembered the fear and concern on her face when she thought I was going to fall. I wanted to see it again so I stopped walking on the fence and started shaking my legs so the fence began to wobble. I knew She couldn't tell that I was doing it on purpose.

"Be careful, Buddy!" she screamed. "Don't fall!"

When I heard the anxiety in Her voice, I just had to look back to see the look on Her face. I just meant to glance at Her but She was standing a little too far behind me. I was still making the fence wobble as I looked back at Her. Suddenly, I realized that I had turned myself too far backward! I felt the fence begin to crack and felt myself falling fast. I flailed my arms and hands this time in earnest. But it was too little – too late! I came down with a thud. I fell on my back and the wind was suddenly knocked out of me. Unable to breathe, I lay there with my eyes closed trying to get my breath.

"Oh! Buddy! Are you hurt?" she cried in a voice that said she was feeling my pain. She pulled and jerked back a stubborn piece of the fence that refused to come apart until she broke it in two. Then She jumped across the broken fence to get to me.

"Say something! Speak to me, Buddy!" By this time, she was sobbing.

I didn't know which was greater – the pain I felt in my body or the joy I felt in my heart because of her caring. I slowly peeked with one eyelid open and – Wonder of Wonders! There were tears in those big beautiful round eyes. She was crying! And she was crying for me! I was ready to die and go to Heaven because I knew nothing I would ever experience was going to top the love and joy I felt at that moment!

I opened my eyes and my face twisted up in pain as I tried to get up. My breath was coming smoother now. I sat up and rubbed the back of my head. When I brought my hand down, She shrieked! She took my hand and held it. Then I saw the blood! Evidently, when I fell, I cut the back of my head. Feeling back there with my other hand I detected a small bruise. She pulled my hand away and reached behind my head. I could scarcely feel the whisper of a touch as gentle as She was.

Her voice was quiet as She said, "I - I know you are very brave. But, you must understand – I'm not! And you really frightened me when I saw you falling. Please try to be careful – if not for you, then for me. Will you - for me?"

I felt like I was ten feet tall and nothing could have hurt me then. I knew there was nothing I could not or would not do for Her.

"Yes! I'll be careful – for you. I can stand any kind of pain - but yes! *I will be very careful for you,*" I promised with a heart that was lifted as high as the beautiful, endless blue sky.

This caring little Watcher was not able to prevent the fall but She brought to the table all that Buddy needed – Her concern! Oft times it is the moment after the trouble that the Watcher will affect more so than the moment before the pain! But true caring and gracious concern will never be too late whenever it arrives!

CHAPTER 30

MY MOST PRECIOUS MOMENT

A Moment! What is the value of a moment? How does the Eternal God view the worth of a moment? Actually, when it is considered that a moment, no matter how brief, is a space in time, the astute observer and the thinker can readily see that to God a moment can be of paramount importance. For, "In a moment, in the twinkling of an eye...we shall be changed." (<u>Cor. 15:52</u>) In Strong's Exhaustive Concordance #G823, the Greek rendering of the word, "moment" is at-om-os and means "an atom of time." What quality of love can be communicated in a moment of time? What reality of the depth and the riches of love can be conveyed to a twelve-year-old boy in an instant? And would the Watcher of Watchers ensure that a young boy would be privileged to encounter his Most Precious Moment in a singular and unique "atom of time?"

Who knew that today would be one of those "THE DAY" days? Oh, you really don't know what a "THE DAY" day is do you? Well, let me fill you in! A "THE DAY" day is a day when something really great happens for the first time.

You know how some really exciting thing happens and years later when you talk about it you talk about "THE DAY" it happened?

Well, for what happened on this day, I should have wakened to a fanfare sounded by one thousand of the greatest trumpeters of the ages! A drum roll played by all of the world's most highly acclaimed drummers since the dawn of time should have been heard as soon as I opened my eyes and was brought to full consciousness! As a matter of fact, not only should I have heard them but so should She, Her mother, my mom and everybody else! For, today I would have an experience that for the rest of my life could be the standard by which all of my most wonderful and exquisite experiences would be judged!

Waking up that Sunday morning, I knew what the agenda was going to be. I was going to wash up, (I had taken my bath the night before) go into the kitchen and eat my breakfast, get dressed and go to church. As I lay there, trying to push myself up and out of bed, I could hear the gospel music on the radio. On Sunday morning the radio was always set on the station, WJLB. This morning I woke to the soulful sound of "The mighty Clouds of Joy." They were followed by "The Five Blind Boys" from Mississippi. It seems like every state in the South had a "Five Blind Boys" quartet. I used to wonder where folks found all of those blind boys because I didn't even know one blind boy, much less a whole quartet.

Anyway, I got up and had to wait my turn to get into the bathroom because I have three brothers and three sisters and it was "first come, first served to get into the bathroom." But my turn finally came. And from there I headed back to the "boy's room." All four of us boys slept in the "boy's room" and my three sisters slept in the "girl's room." I never had my own private bedroom until I moved out at the age of seventeen and that's another story for another day. Now back to this one…!

I might as well confess now that when I walked into the church that day, Jesus was not first and foremost on my mind. You see, ever since I'd had my encounter with Her at the time that I fell off of Junebug's back fence (that was how I got to really know Her), I just couldn't bring myself to face her again. I kept thinking that Her concern for me was probably just a fluke; a onetime thing. I knew that I would rather just have that most exquisite memory than to find out that She just pitied me for falling and hurting myself. But this was Sunday morning and I knew that she would be at Church!

My eyes were peeled to see Her! I am still amazed that a girl, even one as beautiful as this one, could just take over my mind and leave me breathless at just the thought of Her! I mean, I had a picture of Her in my wallet (she didn't know that I had it. I took it with a Polaroid camera I got for Christmas) and sometimes when I went into my wallet to retrieve something, I would unexpectedly come upon Her photo and I do believe that my heart must have skipped a beat!

The church my family attended had about a thousand members. And ever since She came into my life I always sat in the first row of the balcony so that I could find Her more easily. Fortunately, Her Mom always got to church early so She would never have to sit under the balcony. Today I found her family sitting on the right side of the church near the big Hammond organ. She was nestled between her Dad and her

Mom on the third row near the aisle. Her jet black hair was combed to the back in a pony tail that was kind of high up on her head to give it the most perfect arch I had ever seen and in the front her bangs hung just over her eyebrows. With her caramel colored skin, her almond shaped brown eyes and her pert little nose that was slightly turned up on the end, she was oh, so pretty. No! She was passed pretty! She was beautiful! She was wearing a light pink dress with a white collar that matched her white gloves. I used to wonder why the ladies and the girls in the church would wear gloves in the summertime. But today, looking at her, everything she wore was just perfect!

Well, that Sunday morning I really didn't hear much of what the choir sang or said or what the preacher preached or read. All I could see was Her! I saw Her sitting there in the sanctuary but every once in a while, in my mind, I could see her laughing and running through the tall grass in a quiet meadow with a wonderful waterfall in the background (I've always liked waterfalls in pictures). I even saw her sitting next to me on the bank of a slow moving river. And there, she was holding my hand.

Finally, the church service was over and I hurriedly made my way down the stairs and outside through the main double doors. I ran across the street so I could get a better view of the people coming out. It seemed like everybody was pouring out of the doors *but her.*

I was really getting antsy, thinking that I had somehow missed her, when I saw a flash of pink coming through the door. It was really Her! And she seemed to be looking for someone.

"Could she be looking for me?" I hoped. I kept my eyes on her as I took off running back across the street. I had to get there before she could get lost again in the crowd. As I neared her I slowed down so it wouldn't look like I was running to get to Her.

She must have known it was me even before she turned toward me because She was saying, "Hi, Buddy," even as she turned around toward me.

"Hi," I answered. I was no longer as tongue tied now as I was the first day we talked. Her Mom was walking in front of us and she turned around after hearing her daughter's voice. Looking at me she said, "Buddy, do you know where your mother is?"

"No maam," I answered. "I wasn't sitting with her in church and I haven't seen her yet."

"Well, when you see her; please tell her that I have some ideas about a program for the next Mother's Aid meeting."

"Oh, I certainly will, Maam," I promised.

Just then I heard my Mom's voice calling my name. Her mother heard my Mom's voice too and called to my Mom. When my Mom got there, she and the mother of my Her began to walk toward Her mother's car and our home. She and I stepped in behind them and I could hardly believe it but I was actually walking Her to Her car!

It's funny, now that I think about it; I can't remember one thing that we talked about that day! However, I do remember that Her perfume smelled so good. And I remember the sound of the taps on her patent leather shoes on the sidewalk. I remember how Her ponytail swung gracefully from side to side in rhythm with our footsteps. And to, I remember how white Her knee socks and gloves were.

I wonder why we didn't look at each other unless we thought the other wasn't looking. I mean, She would look at me kind of sideways when She thought I was looking the other way! And I would try to steal a glance at Her the same way. I even wondered then if Her reason for not daring to look me straight in the face was because She really liked me and didn't want to be too obvious.

I remember thinking that I was glad that I had worn my Easter suit that day. It was a dark blue Bat Masterson suit, double breasted with two closely set rows of gold colored buttons down the front. It was topped off with a soft black velvet collar. I was also glad that I had polished my shoes last night until they shone like black glass. All day long I had been careful not to get them scuffed or stepped on. I knew that we looked good walking down the street together.

What is also strange is that I had not had a thought all day long about being seen by the Posse, or anybody! All I thought about was Her! But, for a moment, the thought filled my mind that, "I wish the guys and my brother, Jay, could have seen me walking with Her!" I know that I would never have been embarrassed again about being seen with Her! And if being with Her meant that I would have been kicked out of the Posse, then so be it! I would choose her over the Posse any and every day! As a matter of fact, I would have loved to be able to tell Her that I had to pay the cost of being kicked out of the Posse because I had chosen Her over all of them!

When I think back on that day and remember that walk, sometimes I think that walk was the longest short walk that

I ever walked and sometimes it seems to be the shortest long walk I ever walked! But I never really forgot that ONE DAY I WALKED THAT WALK!

Just as all things must, the walk eventually came to an end. And if I thought that all of the events up to that moment were wonderful, I was in no way prepared for what happened next! We got to the corner and my house was across the street. Their car was on the same side of the street that we walked on. When we got to their car, my Mom and Her Mom walked around the car to the driver's side to say their goodbyes. And standing on the grass by the curb, on the passenger's side, I reached over and opened the door for Her! My heart was so happy because I was not just opening the door with my hand; I was opening the door with all of my love that was just gushing out at that moment. Did you know that love has hands that can touch things? Well, it really does! My hands seemed not to have waited for my mind to direct them! They had been poised and ready to do something for Her ever since I woke up that morning! And when we got to the car they just seemed to do what they had been there to do all the day long!

But, even that was no match for the what followed! When I turned around to Her with the car door standing wide opened, She looked me directly in my face and Her eyes found mine! Her most beautiful brown eyes looked straight into mine for a long moment! And what a moment that was! For, in that moment, we created a world all our own! You know, I believe I heard the sound of cascading waterfalls, and saw all of the colors of a rainbow surrounding Her face! I do know that in that moment, I knew the love of every love story that had ever been written! Indeed, for that moment, nothing mattered! There were no wars anywhere in our world. There were no sounds save for the beating of our hearts and I knew that the reason that I could sense no other joys anywhere in our world was because ours was eclipsing all joys!

All of that was more than wonderful but the Wonder of all Wonders occurred when, while still looking into my eyes and saying more than my heart had ever felt, she did that which was beyond any imaginings that my mind had ever created! She reached out just before she got into her car and She squeezed my hand! SHE SQUEEZED MY HAND! I declare, my socks must have rolled up and down! As her mother drove away, my She never looked back! I know because I would have seen Her, for my eyes were transfixed on Her window! I don't know just when my other hand reached over to hold, support and favor the blessed hand but I do remember standing there knowing that I would never wash that hand again! For days I felt or imagined that I felt, that tender gossamer touch! For days I relived that moment when I had actually felt the caress of Heaven's angelic finger! And I know that for all of my life I will remember, THE DAY of "My Most Precious Moment!"

It is true that "…we have not an high priest which cannot be touched with the feeling <u>of our infirmities</u>. (Heb. 4:15)" Since that is true, is it be a stretch of the imagination to perceive that our Master Watcher is also "touched with the feelings of <u>our joy and happiness?</u>" Only a heart of Love can care about and can discern the goings on in a loving heart. Buddy has a loving heart that is able to give and receive love and the Master Watcher will never allow that heart to be devoid of love.

CHAPTER 31

BUDDY'S FEARS

Few negative things are out of the realm of possibility when Satan is writing the mental and spiritual script. Positive reality and negative unreality become meshed in a diabolical conundrum and (gullible) believers are left believing the unbelievable unreality. The following true story (it happened to me) emphasizes the terrible fear that can result when there is no one available to watch over, give clarity or at the very least give courage to a little boy.

It was a cool Indian summer night. The moon was shining in all its nightly glory. The twinkling stars looked like sparkling diamonds against a field of dark blue velvet. All was quiet, save for the occasional cough of Nemo, the big black Doberman next door and the sound of Buddy's brothers and sisters playing in the house.

Twelve-year old Buddy came out of the house and sat down on the steps. He had readily obeyed when his mother asked him to go to the store. He was glad to get out of the house where the heat from the stove in the kitchen had turned every room in the house into a sweat room. His mother (the best cook in the whole church) was cooking for a bake sale.

The soft wind that brushed his face, licked at the tiny beads of perspiration on his forehead. That really felt good!

Buddy usually liked the night. He would often get up in the middle of the night, go outside and sit on the front steps. He used to watch the moths and other bugs that swarmed around the street lamp just two houses from his on the corner of Clinton and Dubois streets. When he heard a car engine start up on the next street, Buddy always liked to imagine where the car was going and who was driving at that time of night.

He would laugh as he heard his oldest sister stumbling around in the dark trying to make her way to the bathroom. She would always bump into something or knock something over. He never understood why she could not remember where everything was.

Sometime during the night, if he waited long enough, old Brother Clay would come down the middle of the street. He would always be preaching or singing at the top of his voice. Brother Clay went to the same church Buddy attended. None of the kids knew where Brother Clay lived but they all saw him down on the railroad tracks all the time, so they thought he was just a hobo. Everybody knew that he had been shell shocked (whatever that meant) in the Korean War.

Yes, Buddy really liked the nighttime in his neighborhood. He looked across the street at old Mrs. Lovely Flowers' house and briefly wondered for the umpteenth time if she was really an old witch who never slept. Staring at her front window, Buddy thought he saw her curtain move. He felt a shiver go down his back as he wondered if she had caught him staring at her. Looking back at his front door, he thought about going back inside his house. He squashed that idea because he remembered that Momma had told him to hurry to the store and buy a pound of butter so she could bake the cake for the church bake sale.

"How come everything looks so different tonight?" Buddy wondered as he started down the porch steps. The trees all seemed to be large monsters whose moving "arms" seemed to be inviting him to his doom. The automobiles that were parked at the curb looked like lurking beasts in the dark! They had headlights that seemed to be great round eyes that pretended to be asleep so that the beasts themselves could pounce on him as he walked by.

Now, Buddy was no one's coward. While watching TV, hadn't he fought bank robbers with Wyatt Earp, the greatest lawman and fastest gun who had ever lived? Hadn't he fought the fierce Blinzenbites with that spaceman, Flash Gordon, on the planet X-phozen every afternoon on TV and wasn't he the only one in his class who dared to blow bubbles in his carton of milk while mean old Mr. "Talk-Through-His-Teeth" Smith was on lunch duty?

Buddy stepped down the last step to the sidewalk and started toward the Colored Store at the corner of Monroe and Chene Streets. Buddy couldn't help but hear sounds from the TV set when he passed his friend, Wobble's house. The guys all called him Wobbles because he was fat and wobbled when he walked. He passed Junebug's house and heard his friend laughing. He thought about asking Junebug if he would go to the store with him, but he knew, if he did, Junebug would think he was scared of the dark and of the scary sounds of the night.

Buddy tried to concentrate on happy thoughts. He tried to remember what the street looked light in the daytime, but try as he might, he couldn't remember the brightness of the sun enough to get rid of the terrible darkness and chase to all the ominous shadows away!

He turned and looked behind himself. He thought he had heard something that sounded like footsteps! He stopped and listened. All was quiet. Nothing looked different than before. He started walking again.

"What was that?" he asked himself. Someone *was* following him! He knew he had heard the unmistakable sound of footsteps that time! He walked slowly, looking straight ahead and suddenly he stopped and whirled around to catch whomever it was that was following him. But all he saw was the empty sidewalk and the empty street. Buddy walked faster. The footsteps got faster! He stopped! They stopped!

Buddy panicked! Forgotten were the times he fought side by side with Wyatt Earp. Lost in his fears were the memories of the battles fought and won at the side of Flash Gordon! All Buddy could think of was not being eaten alive by the monsters, aliens or the dreaded, "Whatevers!" He would have turned around and run back home – but whatever was chasing him was between him and home!

Then Buddy forgot all about caring if anyone knew he was afraid. He balled his little fists up, threw his curly head back and ran as fast as his twelve-year old legs could carry him! But no matter how fast he ran, the footsteps kept pace with him!

He was one of the fastest runners in his class! He wondered who it was he couldn't outrun! He knew it wasn't anybody in his class because he was running faster than he had ever run before! Buddy ran so fast that the tails of his shirt came completely out of his blue jeans! He thought his lungs would burst; that his heart would give out the monster would catch him after all!

Finally, he rounded the corner of Chene and Clinton streets. He had only two more blocks to go! When he saw the lights of the store, he put on a final burst of speed. He ran those two blocks and hit the door to the store in full stride. He didn't stop running until he was halfway to the back of the store, down the cookies and crackers aisle.

Buddy stopped running. He was panting and gasping for breath. He unbuttoned the top button of his shirt and leaned against the shelves. It felt so good to be safe inside the store with its bright lights. And best of all, there were people – friendly people.

He stood there for about five minutes. When he could breathe easily, he remembered that his mother had sent him to the store for a pound of butter. He walked toward the far end of the aisle a*nd he heard footsteps again*! His heart began to race. He walked faster! The footsteps got faster! As he walked faster he looked behind him to catch a glimpse of the man or monster that was threatening his life. He still heard the footsteps but realized that *the aisle was empty*! He turned quickly and looked behind him. But – no one was there! Buddy leaned back against the Keebler cookie shelf. Pressing himself as close to the shelf as he could without knocking any of the boxes down, Buddy waited ready to run if anyone came around the corner. He waited a long minute. Nobody came. He walked faster still! The footsteps sounded faster – *but no one was there!*

Then Buddy looked down at his feet. He smiled! Then from relief as well as joy – Buddy started laughing! He laughed and he laughed and he laughed! He laughed so hard that he couldn't stand any longer. Buddy sat down on the floor and pointed at his shoes and laughed and laughed and laughed! He laughed so hard because he realized that neither monsters, aliens nor the dreaded, "Whatevers" were chasing him! The footsteps that were following him were his own! The soles of his shoes had come loose and were flapping with every step he took! A split second after he took a *step had he heard the flapping of the soles of his own shoes! Buddy had been running away from his own footsteps all the time!*

It should be understood that Buddy was familiar with his neighborhood and was accustomed to feeling safe there. He went to school there, he played there and worshipped there. He lived there! In the daylight there were neither fierce aliens nor monsters or dreaded "Whatevers" to consider. The result of Buddy's fears was that he was left tired from running and eventually relieved that his fears were unfounded. He even had a great laugh about his adventure.

However, in the life of the Christian, the stakes are infinitely higher. Many fearful ones are left spiritually maimed and scarred by the effects of fear. As a matter of fact, John, the Revelator, asserts, "But the fearful, and unbelieving, and the abominable, and murderers, and whoremongers, and sorcerers, and idolaters, and all liars, shall have their part in the lake which burneth with fire and brimstone: which is the second death." (Rev. 21:8)

Please note that the fearful and unbelieving are put in some very bad company in God's estimation. You must fight fear with every weapon and every ounce of strength you can muster because fear is actually the devil's attempt to get you to redefine God. His intended result is that you lower your estimation of God so that you become children of a lesser god! Hence, the need for Watchers!

CHAPTER 32

AN ANGEL FOR A TEN-YEAR OLD

It is very important that children learn at an early age to have noble feelings and to express then appropriately. In this story, the Master Watcher has designed that a very creative and imaginative youngster is filled with ideas of caring and affection. The little one who is the devotee in this story doesn't know just how to be devoted but he learns that pure honesty and sincerity will win out in the end; a lesson that only the Wisdom of God can teach.

It was the last Friday of Vacation Bible School in the summer of '53. I was ten years old and I was in a mess of a problem! What I had been thinking for the last week and a half went against everything I believed in. You see, I had been thinking about Her. And what is worse, in my mind I have been calling her "My Alexis!"

Alexis! *My* Alexis! Oh, you don't know about her. Do you? Well, let me tell you! Nobody in our neighborhood, in our school or even in our church had ever been named, "Alexis!" It was like she came from Europe, maybe England or Germany!

You know, somewhere far away where the names were not Alice or Betty or Annie. Later on, after I really got to know her, I realized that most of our friends called her "Lexie." But there was no way that I was going to disrespect her name by giving it all of the dignity of a slang word! No! To me she will never be a "Lexie!" She would ever remain a cut above all of the rest of the ordinary and everyday girls! I would never put her in the same category of a Dee Dee or a Debby or even a Barb! She will always be the very grand and lovely, "Alexis!"

From the first time I laid eyes on her my world began to unravel at some very important edges. I mean, just the week before, at the last Posse meeting, all of the guys had all renewed our vow to have nothing to do with girls. We didn't like them, didn't play with them and didn't ask them for anything - excepting moms, of course. The boys in my neighborhood, who played together every day called ourselves the "Posse." Western TV shows were big back then.

When she came into our classroom at Vacation Bible School, Alexis kind of just stood for a moment in the doorway. The sunlight from the open door of the classroom across the hall was almost blinding. As she stood in the doorway, her outline had a brightness that made her glow like an angel. She walked slowly into the room and as she came through the doorway and away from the sunlight, her features became more visible. I can see her now in my mind. Her hair was jet black and her brown eyes were the shape of perfect little almonds. I remember thinking that her skin was the color of brown sugar.

She looked around the room for an empty seat and saw the one right next to me. My heart must have skipped a beat as I smiled at her in an obvious invitation. Then she looked at me and I saw her look around for another seat. She found one all the way over at the farthest corner of the room.

What had just happened? And why was I so hurt? Did anybody know what had happened? I looked around at the other kids but they were busy doing whatever they were before she opened the door. I looked back at the picture of Noah's ark that I was coloring when she opened the door but, try as I might, I couldn't get her out of my mind!

So, for more than a week I had been thinking about her. Half the time I was scared that the Posse, my oldest brother, Jay or somebody was going to notice that I was really noticing her! My great problem was that I just didn't know what to do about her! The rare times when she said something to me usually found me too tongue tied to respond and at other times my mouth got dry all of a sudden like I had swallowed a mouth full of sawdust! It went on that way too long, with me hoping that she would speak to me and me being so full of fear that she would! I knew I had to get some help!

The source of the best help that was available to me was my oldest brother, Jay. Now, you've got to understand why Jay was the most likely choice for my advisor! He was eleven years old and was simply the smartest kid I knew! He even entered a story in the Duffield Elementary School writing contest! And he won! He was awarded a big beautiful fairy tale storybook! Plus, he was the fastest runner in our neighborhood and he could even whistle through his two baby fingers so shrilly that you could hear him more than four blocks away! And I have never asked him a question that he couldn't answer!

I went to his classroom, looked through his door window and beckoned him out into the hall. He must have told his teacher that he had to go to the bathroom or something because a couple of minutes later he was out in the hall with me.

"What's up, Buddy?" he asked.

"Uh., Jay, uh…" was as far as I got.

"Hurry up, Buddy," he demanded. "I can't be out here all day!"

I knew that he was not going to stay out in that hall with me for long so I just came out with it.

"Jay, what should you do when you like a girl?"

"Buddy, I thought that you didn't like girls!" Jay remarked with a of knowing grin on his face.

"I…I don't like *girls,* Jay. *But I like liking this girl!*"

He punched me on my shoulder and said, "My kid brother is finally growing up!"

"C'mon, Jay," I said. "What are you supposed to do when you like a girl in a special and kinda' stupid and wonderful way?"

"You just tell her, Buddy." he replied and I knew that Jay understood me.

"Just like that?" I ask.

"Just like that!" Jay said.

He went back into his classroom and I went back to mine! The reason that it was so important that I ask Jay my question was my class was going to go to recess when I got back to the room. I knew that when we went to recess the first place the girls were going was to the restroom. The restrooms were down in the basement where the prayer rooms and other classrooms were. My plan was to go to the drinking fountain that was a few feet from the girl's restroom and I was going to drink water from that fountain until she came out.

Sure enough, when I got back to class our teacher sent us to recess. I let everybody leave the room before I went out. I knew that the boys were going out to the parking lot to play football. So, I was not worried about being seen by them. And with the girls in the bathroom, I had a good chance of catching her by herself.

What I didn't know was that by the time we went to recess it was raining buckets outside! When I got to the basement, all of the teachers and the boy and girls were milling around in there like so many sheep! I truly did not want to take the risk that anybody would know how I felt about her but *this was the last day of Vacation Bible school!* And I knew that I couldn't let her go away without telling her what I felt about Her! It wasn't what she felt about me that mattered but what I felt about her! I know that I wanted Her to like me but that would have really been the icing on the cake!

I went to the drinking fountain and drank as slowly as I could. I made a big noise, slurping and sucking (more air than water) because I didn't want the adults to think that I was just standing around the girl's restroom. Soon, a girl came out. Then groups of two or three starting coming out. But not her!

Despite the fact that I was drinking as slowly as possible, I eventually began to feel water logged! I mean, you can only drink so much water! Just about the time that I thought I might have to give up, She came out! I let her get just past me while I quickly wiped the water from my mouth with my shirt sleeve.

"Hey!" I said to her. She looked around and stopped. I ran over to her and tried to talk but the words seemed to be jammed down my throat!

"I...." Nothing else came out! "I..., uh...." Still more nothing!

"What, Buddy," she asked in a voice that sounded like one beautiful and oh, so perfect angel.

I had never heard my name sound so wonderful, so musical, so personal! I knew that I had to say something! I could not stand there one second more looking silly in the presence of her glorious beauty!

I quickly made up my mind that I was going to get these words out if I had to burst trying! So I took a deep breath and demanded the words to COME OUT OF MY MOUTH!

"I...I... I LOVE YOU!" I shouted! The words not only came out of my mouth! They filled the entire basement! Everybody heard me. The teaching staff, the girls and all of the boys! She looked at me and for a fleeting instant I thought I saw the makings of a smile before she ran out of the basement and up the stairs!

Oh! How they laughed! Grownups laughed saying how cute it was! The girls laughed and envied her! The boys laughed, thinking that I was up to one of my pranks again! For their own reasons they laughed! They all laughed!

They were not, however, the focus of my thoughts! My embarrassment was conflicting with my concern for her! Did she really start to smile or was she just beginning to frown? Was she angry or was she happy? How can I face anyone again? Wil I be the butt of every joke? I did not want to know what I knew I must find out! Very quickly the negative certainty won out over the positive hope!

I walked back to the classroom knowing that I would be alone there because none of the kids ever wanted recess to end. Most of them straggled in just a little late. I walked up the long hallway to the classroom with my head bowed in miserable defeat. I opened the door and as I walked to my desk, hot tears of hopes crushed began their cascading descent down my cheeks. At that moment, tears came as only the innocent and unsophisticated can shed them. My budding love was dying on the vine of my heart and causing tears to break through the fragile lids of my eyes! At my desk, I sat and was just starting to lay my head down when I sensed a presence near me. I raised my head and looked to the desk next to mine that had been empty all of this time and saw the Wonder of all Wonders! Sitting there in all of her (I didn't know this word then) *exquisite* glory and most excellent beauty was she, the love of my heart! And as I looked at her, she looked at me and she finished the smile she had begun at our moment in the basement!

CHAPTER 33

THE MAN BEHIND PAPER THIN WALLS!

There may be no better motivation than the devotion that is bred in the heart of a loving spouse. Hence, there may be no more devoted and courageous Watcher than the vigilant spouse! The love of the Watchers in this story is marvelous! It actually causes these married lovers to vie for the opportunity to risk life, limb and feelings for one another. Such is the nature of all of those who have found a oneness in their love.

Picture it! The summer of '53! It was one of those sweltering hot days in the city of Detroit, Michigan. My name is Buddy Tolbert. I was about nine years old at the time and at the moment I had nothing to do. So, I got an old Sunday newspaper that was in a stack on the trunk on the back porch and to my delight it still had the comic strip in it. I loved to read, Dick Tracy, the Phantom, Beetle Bailey and almost all of the rest.

There was no breeze, no wind, no air conditioning, no fan, nothing as I placed the newspaper on the floor, turned to the funnies and began to smooth out the pages. Just as I was lying down on the floor I heard footsteps coming up on the porch. The main door was wide open to let in any wayward breeze that might accidently pass by. But the screen door was locked! And I was so glad that it was locked when I saw who it was! I got up and started toward my Dad and Mom's bedroom door to tell them that the landlord was at the door.

Now, you've got to understand something about this man. He was what we called "of the Caucasian persuasion" and he did not care one bit that we were renting this house from him! He said that the house was his; in his name and he didn't have to knock on his door! If the screen door had been unlatched, he would have just walked right on in! But to my great satisfaction *this time it was locked!*

I walked over to the bedroom door and announced, "Dad, Mom, Mr. So-in-so is here!" I don't remember the man's name. I didn't know it then but there was an issue that made today's landlord visit a singular and unique one! And this situation had to be handled delicately! For some reasons, my Dad and Mom didn't have all of the rent money!

Through those paper thin walls, I heard my Dad say, "I'll go talk to him!" My mother replied, "Now, Samuel, you know that I have to go!" To which my Daddy said, No, Grace, this time I'll go!"

"Samuel, you know *I've got to go and talk to him!*" my mother reasoned insistently.

You see, back in those days the Black man had to be strong enough to make himself weak at a time when his strength could have been destructive! We knew this because we had been taught that the more decent White man would usually accord the Black woman more deference, honor and respect than her male counterpart. In those days, our landlord, being as insensitive and uncaring about our feelings as he was, might have called my father the "N" word or he could have even killed him if my Dad made any show of force or resistance or if the man had in anyway perceived signs that he interpreted as disrespect. And make no mistake about it - not much would have been done to give my family justice!

Be sure you understand that, my father was a peaceable man and always sought to present Jesus in the best light, *he was not a weak man!* This was just about survival! I'm glad that he had the strength to show restraint! For, my Dad taught his children that *"The strongest man in the world may not be the one who can pick up the most weight – it may well be the man who can control his strength best!"*

Well, to get back to the story, the rent was forty dollars a month but that was a lot of money to a lot of folks back then. Soon, my Mom came out of the bedroom, gave the man the amount that we had and made arrangements to pay the rest. The landlord left and then she latched the screen door and walked back to her bedroom. It was then, through those "paper thin walls" that I heard a conversation I would remember and deal with for many years to come.

I can never think of this episode in my life without feeling layers of emotion when I come to this part. I had just begun to read the comics again when I heard my Dad say, "But, I am *a man!"* And my Mom answered, "Yes, Samuel, you are a man!"

Dad, then said, "But I AM a man!"

Mom again agreed, "Yes, Samuel, you are my man!" I AM A MAN, GRACE!" Dad exclaimed.

Mom replied in a way that was patently hers; in her voice that was always so comforting and reassuring, "You are much of a man, Samuel and you are still alive and you're well and I'm so proud of you! And you know how much I love you!"

Then, I heard my father asked a question of my mother that was probably asked in the deepest echelons of Colored men all across these United Sates of America - *to no avail!* I can imagine Colored men of all hues and ages in varying stages of life, questioning God, themselves and whoever would entertain the thought! Some of these may have stared questioningly up into the darkness that has existed since before the dawning of time; a darkness that *should have known the answer!* Some may have lain in confusion on their beds of dirt or their mattresses of straw or corn shucks or even on their Broyhill beds with their Posterpedic mattresses in the blackness that had seen all of life unfold in its presence the darkness that *should know this answer!* But, frustratingly, the strangely quiet darkness proved to be as much in the dark concerning this issue as was all else of creation; this dark that revealed nothing despite its inestimable age! How many slaves before, during and after the antebellum period of American history, as well as freed men during and after the end of the Civil War entertained this elusive question? What is the number that has either by means of conscious thought or by the fancy of a dream in the deep solitude of their nocturnal reflections, queried this notion? Who were they that sought to see through the oblivion of the dark in this darkness to the revelation that would give light to this haunting and necessary question? How many were the times when Colored men wondered this elusive thought with furrowed brows and mahogany skin that was leathery from following the plow or from some other such labor in the heat of the sun, the driving rain and the freezing cold? Did they speculate and question this seemingly unfathomable issue as they gazed down into the innocent and trusting faces of their sons when the query, *"When will they let me be a man?"* broke through to the fore of their minds? I have seen them both in my personal experience and in my mind's eye when they sought to be hired on a job that they were imminently qualified for but were denied and left with only their frustrations and longings and questions! It seems that in my quiet musings, I have heard Black men who were noble and good, intelligent and skilled, loving and caring, cry out in the interminable darkness and the abysmal depths of their despair - the question that became almost palpable but was left unanswered; times to numerable to mention, "When *will* they let me be a man?"

Even now, I can almost see my Dad look into those eyes of his soulmate, my Mother; into those eyes that always held the promise of the comfort and peace of the wisdom of the ages. I can almost hear him ask her the question that haunted me for many years after. Dad pleaded, *"When will they let me be a man, Gracie?"*

The landlord never allowed himself to see past the hatred and the prejudice that eclipsed all of the beauty, the tenderness and the nobility that were elements in the love that filled the hearts of my Dad and my Mom! Or perhaps he was simply too brutish and insensitive or just plain ignorant and mean, to know that there was more to this issue than he realized?

It is a satisfying portion to those who are sensitively Watched and lovingly protected by a Watcher who honestly and truly, faithfully and purely, Watches! And who truly sees the value of the one he Watches! How often does mankind go through life looking at people whom they never really see?

CHAPTER 34

"HELPING HIM CRY"

This writer finds that God's planning and His grand designs are so perfect in every way that no matter what direction we consider His actions from, the essentiality and the purpose of all parts of a story that God writes falls perfectly into place and are vital to all of the other elements of His narrative. Whether it is from the beginning of a history, the middle of what occurred or from history's end, the story can be appreciated in its entirety.

In this story of Skeeter, his wife, Noel, and little Joey, the notion of there being "No Unguarded Moments" in the lives of God's children most assuredly comes to life. Understanding and receiving this truth into your heart is best accomplished from the vantage point of a most copiously clear realization of the depth, the quality and the purity of God's Love for His family.

He had never felt so alone in his life! And that was because he had never been so alone in his life! Even when their only daughter had died giving birth to their only grandchild - *he had never felt this alone!* And when they found out that their grandchild had been born dead and the last of their daughter's life had died with the baby – *still, he had never been so alone!*

He looked out of the living room window as he headed out to the garage. The day was just like countless others. And that, somehow, seemed wrong on so many levels. On this day, when he would finally put the exclamation point on the fact of his greatest loss ever, he thought that surely there would be something that would declare the uniqueness and the incomparable difference of this day!

This worst of all of the days of his life should, he reasoned, be dark with thunder clouds that threatened the worst rain and hail storm ever! Yes, the sun should have been locked behind heavy clouds that should have been blown hard by cold and heartless winds. He should be hearing the sound of the wind blowing; winds that caused the trees to knock and clack their limbs against one another as if clapping their hands to mock him on this worst of all his days! He felt that he should be hearing the winds scream and groan as if in pain as they cut themselves on the corners of the houses.

But, no! The sun was shining in all of its June morning glory in one of the bluest skies he had ever seen. The Blue Jay that always pestered the squirrels in the big Elm tree in the front yard was giving them a fit as usual. The roses that lined the front of the house were as bright and lovely as ever and his grass never looked greener.

He really didn't think about where he was going. He just got into his car and backed out of his driveway to drive slowly away. When he noticed the roses and the azaleas that were the boundary for the driveway, he thought, "She was so proud of growing her flowers!" Actually, he could barely see them though the curtain of tears that wouldn't stop flowing. He had to squint to see the street in front of his car. As he drove pass the front of his house, he realized that he was going to see her - *for the last time.*

However, it wasn't only his tears that clouded his vision. In his mind he was looking back in time to when he was eight years old and saw her for the first time. She was in the top branches of old Mr. Mallory's apple tree. She was filling a little basket with the biggest and juiciest apples of all! But what first got his attention were the yellow ribbons that were tied around her two long black pigtails. Those yellow ribbons were the only things that were yellow in the tree. He would have had to be almost blind to miss them!

"Hey! Who's up in that tree stealin' old Mr. Mallory's apples?" he had yelled.

"Who's askin'?" She yelled back.

The second thing that caught his eye through the thick leaves was the cutest round face he had ever seen. She was the color of the caramel syrup that he always wanted Mr. Peoples to dribble on his favorite ice cream sundaes down at the drug store. And on her face she had just a tiny sprinkling of freckles that surrounded the cutest dimples he had ever seen. Her pert little nose was turned up ever so slightly on the end. She was so pretty that he just couldn't help staring at her.

"It's me! I've come to cut Mr. Mallory's grass like I do every Saturday!" He replied.

"Well, who is 'Me'?" She demanded. "Everybody is s'pose to have a name!"

"Oh! Sorry. My name is Lester but everybody calls me 'Skeeter!'"

"I'm 'Noel' on account of my momma lovin' Christmas so much. And, by the way, *Skeeter*, I ain't stealin' 'cause this tree belongs to my granddaddy."

"You mean old Mr. Mallory is *your Grandpa?*" Skeeter asked.

"Duh! That's what I just said!" "Hey! Did your Momma have any intelligent kids?" she wanted to know.

He could not explain it but just then he knew he was hooked! He fell head-over-heels in love with her from that moment and he never *ever* stopped loving her!

This puppy love that was to blossom eventually into a full-fledged, bona-fide, genuine, deep and abiding affection, was the foundation and the catalyst for the launching of one of the greatest loves of all time. It also lended itself to Skeeter becoming Noel's most loving and faithful Watcher.

CHAPTER 35

FROM PROM QUEEN TO SOULMATE

We know what we want sometimes better than we know what we need! The former seems to be easier to determine because we simply examine our feelings and appetites! Actually, God, through the pen of Jeremiah observes that "the heart is deceitful above all things, and desperately wicked: who can know it?" Jer. 17:9 KJV So, for man to succinctly and distinctly decide what is best for him is a much more difficult task than one might think.

However, when one's Watcher is the All-seeing Eye of God, the choice is easily made! Remember, God gives His best to those who leave the choice to Him! When one considers the life of Skeeter and Noel that truth becomes readily apparent.

As he drove slowly down the street toward his last time with her, the scene changed in his mind and he was soon seeing her when she was seventeen years old. That was the year she was voted "Prom Queen." When the winners were announced and the time came to dance the special dance, everyone thought she was going to dance with William Simpson, the captain of the football team who had been voted "Prom King." William Simpson had been trying his best to take Noel out on a date for the entire year. He couldn't understand why she refused to go out with him. He was six feet and two inches tall with curly hair and all the girls said he was "hot." Then, he heard that she was going steady with *Skeeter Jenkins!* He just could not believe that she would choose Skeeter over him! Not that he had anything against Skeeter but he knew that he could have his pick of any girl at school! William Simpson just could not see what Skeeter had that he didn't!

To everybody's surprise (but William Simpson's) she left the stage and came to where Skeeter was standing over by the punch bowl and led him out to the dance floor. This was the moment Skeeter knew that he was going to marry Noel!

Somehow, the scene in his mind began to shift again; to change and morph until he saw her coming up the aisle in their church. As he looked back on that moment, his heart swelled with love and pride as he knew that she loved him enough to become his wife.

She was so beautiful in her gossamer white wedding gown. Her hair was so long now that it nearly hung to her waist. He remembered the way she walked so confidently and purposefully. He saw her come down the aisle toward him. As he went to meet her and took her hand, she looked at him so shyly. He remembered wondering how she could come to him so boldly and then at his touch become so timid that she smiled and blushed. But that was just her way. He thought of how she looked up at him when the pastor said, "You may kiss your bride." She was shy again but she lifted her lips to meet his. And he would never doubt, from that moment on, for the rest of her life, that her heart would be totally his. And when the pastor presented Skeeter and Noel to the congregation of well-wishers with the words, "Ladies and gentleman, I present to you Mr. and Mrs. Lester Jenkins," he knew to the core of his being that he had married his "forever friend" and his one and only "soulmate!"

CHAPTER 36

AGING TOGETHER IS AGING AT ITS BEST

Only the All Wise God could have Watched so well and known Skeeter and Noel so completely that He knew that they would age without getting older than one another. And only God could have designed their hearts to appreciate the strength and the wisdom that every stage of their relationship brought to bear. What a wonderful Watcher He is!

The old man was shaken back to the day's reality when his right front tire hit a pothole in the street. Without being aware that he did it, he wiped away tears that were streaming down his face. Old Skeeter looked at the windshield and saw Noel's face just as he had seen it the day before she died. He had brought some of her roses and azaleas to her hospital room in a vase so she could see a touch of home after he had gone for the night. When he bent over the bed and softly called to her to see if she was awake he had paused and looked at her. Her pert little nose that pointed slightly up on the end and her little dimples were still as they were from the first time he had seen her.

Once again, looking at her, he was somewhat amazed how much she had aged. He had not known when Noel began to age but he remembered the day when he noticed the first strands of gray hair just above her ears on both sides of her head. She was standing in the kitchen washing dishes after a Sunday dinner. Walking through the kitchen as he was going to the garage to get his Sunday paper out of the car, he just couldn't resist stopping to give her a little kiss. Skeeter walked up behind her and reached down to give her a peck on the cheek and that's when he saw the gray strands.

When she felt his hands gently around her waist, she turned around, quickly drying her hands on her apron. That's when he saw the little "crow's feet" wrinkles just beginning to form at the corners of her eyes. He thought to himself, "How dare time touch my beautiful Noel! How dare life try to change the perfect beauty of my perfect love?" His next thoughts were, "When had this happened? I have been here all this time and I never saw it happening!"

But something wonderful occurred when he stopped looking at her hair and the wrinkles on her face. It happened when he looked into her big brown eyes. There the real story was told! Those eyes told the real truth! The beauty that she possessed when she was eight years old was the beauty of innocence and childhood wonder. Her beauty at seventeen was the beauty of young life with all the marvels and the splendor of youthful possibilities and potentials. And her beauty during their years of marriage up to that point was the beauty of maturing love, the strength of hope and the joy of growing into the most excellent beauty; the beauty that Skeeter loved with all of his heart. Skeeter realized then that her exquisite loveliness was the beauty of a love that was tested and had endured; a love that was bruised by life but was yet unbowed. It was the beauty of hopes sought after and realized; of worthy battles fought and of victories worn with grace.

Skeeter remembered that she had turned around and with her back to the sink had stood on her tip toes and reached her hands up to bring his face down closer so she could kiss him. For a fleeting moment, *she* noticed that *he had changed.* His walnut brown face was no longer smooth, his eyebrows were now white and his moustache (that she always loved to tickle her when they kissed) was now silver and white as was his full head of hair. His face was no longer just *the color of walnut* but it was gnarled with grooves that seemed to be purposefully etched by a wise and skillful hand. His face was wrinkled from weathering many years of snow, wind and sun.

As she gazed lovingly into his eyes, she was suddenly overcome with the overwhelming understanding that for all of these years that she had known Skeeter, she had been purely and unselfishly loved. She always knew that the crowning touch of her beauty was the result of simply knowing and living in the presence of such a beautiful and wise man as her Skeeter had become!

Noel also knew with every fiber of her being that when she and Skeeter had accepted Christ as their Savior, her Lord had given her two gifts. One was the Gift of Himself filling her heart. Then the Father, God, had taken Skeeter and wrapped him up, in the Love of Jesus Christ as a gift and presented her Skeeter to her. As she loved him then, with her eyes, she understood that though he had grown old, he had not aged altogether. The sparkle still twinkled in his eyes. Though his hands shook, they still touched her with the gentleness and the comfort of his youth. Though his voice was weaker, softer, they spoke with more wisdom and a deeper love than they ever could have when he was young.

CHAPTER 37

THE MOST EXTRAORDINARY ORDINARY DAY

Even though Noel is gone, Skeeter is careful to Watch that he never deviates from the life they lived together. He understands that one of the ways to keep her near him is to continue to do the things that they enjoyed together! But he also refuses to live differently than they did together! They never rose a limo together so he would not ride in one without her! It was not the limousine that was so important but the lack of her presence. Watching himself and keeping the traditions they shared keeps her close to him as nothing else could!

The old man, Skeeter, now had on his best and only suit. Noel had always smiled at him and said that he looked like a "Philadelphia lawyer" when he wore his suit. But he never thought so. He had always thought himself to be a simple man who never needed the flashy clothes that other men needed so as to be thought distinguished and successful. Even when he was a young man he wore clothes that helped him to blend into the background of a room. So, for this very special day, he dressed in his black suit, a white shirt, a skinny black tie and his black lace up shoes.

For some reason, he wanted this day to be just a regular day even though he knew that he had never lived a day like this one before and he knew he would never live a day like this one again. He didn't think anyone would understand it but it was important to him that this extraordinary day be *just another day.* He thought that if he could make this day seem to be just another day, maybe, just maybe, it would seem to him that she was still nearby. He wanted to feel that she was close to him even though he knew that she had never been as far away from him as she now was and would always be until the day he would go to her.

But there was one very strangely wonderful thing that he knew was very real in his heart! Skeeter knew that he would never feel his arms around her again or be warmed in the radiance of her smile. And despite the fact that he would no longer be both comforted and excited by the love in her eyes - he knew that Noel would never be far from him because she had a permanent place in the hollow of his heart. In his mind he could even now hear her calling his name as only she could, with a voice that both invited him and compelled him to give all of his attention to her.

The funeral director had wanted to have him picked up in a limousine and driven to the church. But he said, "No, thank you. I'll just drive myself." He had never ridden in a limousine with Noel and he just couldn't ride in one without her being with him - especially on this extraordinary, but ordinary, day!

When he left the house in his own car to go the funeral, he tried to pretend that it was a Sunday morning and she was sitting next to him in the car and they were just going to church. But because of the time of day, he knew that they couldn't be going to Sunday school. No! They were just going to Morning Worship.

CHAPTER 38

THE WORST TEARS TO CRY – LONELY TEARS ALONE

It is not unlikely that God will allow a hardship to be experienced in order that a greater good can be accomplished. In John 11:14-15 KJV, speaking to His disciples, Jesus declared, "Lazarus is dead. And I am glad for your sakes that I was not there, to the intent that you may believe…." Similarly, God permitted little Joey's puppy, Sparky to die that Joey might learn the compassion that was needed to comfort old Skeeter in his time of distress. What a wonderful Watcher Jesus is!

His name was, Joey. The seven-year-old little boy was sitting on the swing at the park. His baseball cap that covered his mini afro was at an angle to the left side of his head. His red and white striped tee shirt hung down outside of his blue jeans that had a hole in both knees. Joey's sneakers were worn and comfortable. His sling shot hung from his back pocket ready to be used to knock a can off a fence or clang against a stop sign.

All the kids Joey had been playing with were gone home and the mothers who walked their babies in the park had left for the day. Those who exercised themselves and those who exercised their dogs had gone. The only person in the park was little Joey. He didn't know what time it was and he really didn't care just then.

Joey wasn't swinging. He was just sitting there. He just couldn't stop thinking of his little Cocker Spaniel, Sparky. He was remembering when his Dad and Mom had asked him what he wanted for his birthday two years ago. They had asked him a week before his birthday and he had taken his time thinking before he gave his answer. That was just his way! Joey didn't give quick answers to questions that were important. He had to think and re-think his answers because he knew that sometimes you only got one shot at getting just what you really wanted. After three days of thinking and re-thinking he made his decision! At first he thought he wanted a new first baseman's glove. But that wouldn't be much fun to play with unless he had someone to throw the ball to him so he squashed that idea. Everything he thought of, he knew would be more fun playing with someone else. He didn't have any brothers and sisters and he just couldn't ask for a new baby brother because it would be years before a new brother would be big enough to play with him. So little Joey thought and thought and thought some more. Then, like a bolt of lightning it hit him! What he needed was a dog; a dog that would be his alone and love him and play with him and be his friend!

When he told his parents, they were not so enthusiastic about the idea because they didn't want to have to feed the dog and walk him and clean up after him! What they didn't know was that he wanted to do all those things for his dog himself because that's what would make the dog his more than anything else would. So, he promised to take care of the dog all by himself. That did it! They agreed. Next, they asked him where he wanted to go to get the dog.

"I don't know," answered Joey. "I guess from a dog store." His father grinned at him and said, "I mean would you rather buy a dog from a Pet store or would you rather get one from a dog pound?"

"What difference would it make?" Joey replied, "I will still be getting a dog no matter where it comes from."

"Well, it does make a difference, Son, because if we get a dog from the Dog Pound we may be saving the dog's life. You see, Joey, some dog pounds don't have the money to keep dogs for long periods of time so they "put them down" after a certain period of time."

"What does *put them down* mean, Dad?" asked the little seven-year-old. "Well, Joey, that means to put them to sleep by giving them something that will cause them to never wake up," Dad said.

"You meant that they will kill a dog if we don't go to the Dog Pound and get it?" cried Joey with a look of horror all over his face! His mind was made up then and the next day they went to the Dog Pound to pick out his new friend.

When they entered the Pound, the noise was so loud! They heard all kinds of barks. They heard the short high pitched, "Yip, yip" and the deep voiced, "Woof, woof." Then there was the long drawn out, "Arrooough, Arrooough!" They even heard the "Meowing" from the cats and the kittens on the other side of a wall.

A lady who looked very nice and friendly was standing behind the counter refilling a jar with some doggie treats.

"May I help you," she asked in her very sing songy voice.

"Yes Maam," little Joey piped up excitedly. "Tomorrow is my birthday and I'll be eight years old and my mommy and my daddy asked me what I want for my birthday and I thought about it and thought about it and thought about it and then it just came to me out of the blue – I want a dog and *here I am!*"

Joey thought the nice lady was super nice when she took him by his hand and led him back through some double doors into the kennel where all of the dogs were. Joey had never seen so many dogs before! There were little dogs and big dogs, black dogs, white and brown dogs. There were furry dogs and long hair dogs and short hair and curly haired dogs. White dogs with black spots were there and black dogs with white spots were there. But of all the dogs that Joey saw and liked, there was a short, black and white one with hair that was curly *and straight*. And he had a black circle on his back just around his tail where it began. His little ears were pointed and his little pink tongue was sticking out of his mouth so that he appeared to be laughing at the funniest joke that was ever told.

So it was that Sparky came home to live with Joey. Sparky became his favorite pal. Soon, he walked Joey to the bus stop every morning and waited with him until the bus picked him up. And somehow, Sparky just knew when it was time for the bus to bring Joey home. So, he was always waiting at the bus stop for the little guy.

Little Joey wasn't thinking of those things though, while he sat on the swing at the playground. He was thinking that *he was never going to play with Sparky again!* He and Sparky would never share an ice cream cone again. Sparky would never again chase another ball nor sleep in Joey's bed. He would never wake his little boy pal again by licking his face. These things could never happen again because last week little Sparky was hit by a car when he ran out into the street chasing a squirrel. The squirrel made it across *but Sparky didn't.* By the time the little boy ran over to him, *Sparky was already dead.*

Joey had never felt a pain so bad and had never cried so much as he did that day! He felt that he could never be happy again. Who would walk him to school and be at the bus stop when he came home? Who would snuggle close to him at night when he heard *The Boogie Man* under his bed? Who would understand the things he had to say that grownups couldn't? Who would lick the tears from his face when he was sad? Sparky could never again do all the things that were so important to a seven-year-old kid and there was no one to take his place! So, Joey had cried the worst and hardest of all of the tears anyone could ever cry – lonely tears alone!

CHAPTER 39

THE CALL OF SADNESS
SHOULD NEVER BE DENIED

Quite often, people, especially men. Feel that they can go it alone; that they don't need any help. But the Wisdom and Compassion of God always provides that there is a strength nearby to help anyway. Today, Skeeter who prided himself on being able to handle whatever comes his way doesn't realize that his Lord has seen to it that someone, a Watcher, is on board to help carry his load and burden of grief.

"No! Skeeter, you are most certainly not alone in this time of your greatest loneliness! Little Joey is here! And he is here to help!"

Old Skeeter stopped the car and sat there for just a moment. He took the car key out of the ignition, unfastened his seatbelt and opened the door. He half climbed out and half fell out onto the street. The old man walked across the street and entered the park. He was barely aware of where he was. He didn't realize that he had come to *her favorite place.* Noel used to love to come to the park and watch the people; the exercisers and the dog walkers, the lovers holding hands and the children playing. She loved the whole park scene. Without knowing it, Skeeter had come to the last place they had enjoyed together.

Old Skeeter's suit was now all wrinkled and rumpled. His tie was loose and one of his shoes had come unlaced. But he didn't know it. He stumbled into the park and headed to their favorite park bench. In his mind, he saw the scene they last saw together. He heard the children laughing, the birds chirping and the squirrels chattering and fussing at one another. In his mind's eye the old man saw the children running through the park, playing on the merry-go-round, climbing the monkey bars and swinging on the swings. Skeeter heard the children laughing and the girls squealing as they love to do so much. He heard a kid shout out, "You're it!" as a game of tag was played in Skeeter's mind. In his mind, lovers were there, unmindful and uncaring about anything and anyone but themselves as they walked hand in hand, seeing and hearing what no one else could for they were, after all, in love.

The old man squinted his eyes and looked for *their* bench. He found it over near the swings under the old Oak tree and walked slowly over to the bench and sat down.

As Little Joey sat on the swing he saw the old man shuffle into the park and head right where Joey knew he would. He didn't know him but he remembered seeing the old man and his wife at the park. He had seen them almost every time he came there. He thought that it was strange to see him without her. But as he watched the old man, he noticed that the old man's shoulders were shaking. Then the little boy thought he heard a sound that he had never heard before coming from the old man. It was a sound that was familiar to him although he knew he was hearing it for the first time coming from that source. Then it came to him! The sound that he recognized was the sound of sadness and crying. The old man was crying as if something in him was tearing him apart. He was sobbing. He was grieving as if something or someone very special to him had died!

The little boy remembered how he had felt and cried when his little pal, Sparky, died. Young Joey knew the hurt that the old man felt. He knew that pain! He knew that sadness! He knew that loneliness. And something stirred in the heart of the little boy named Joey because he knew how hard it is to cry alone! So, he knew what he had to do!

The little guy got down from the swing and walked over past the merry-go-round to the bench where the old man wept. He stood in front of the old man for a moment. Old Skeeter didn't even know Joey was there! He didn't hear him walk up and he certainly couldn't see him through the tears that blurred his eyes.

Then, because his legs were so short, Joey had to climb up on the far end of the bench, close but not too close, to the old man and there he sat down. As he sat there, he could feel the bench shake as the old man cried. He heard the sad groaning of the old man's voice and in those groanings he heard the sound of memories that could be lived no more. He heard the sound of joys that could no longer be enjoyed. He heard the sound of laughter that would never be heard on the winds again. And even in his little eight-year-old mind he could hear the echoes of a love and a promise of love that he knew would not be denied! Joey sensed that though the old man couldn't know it today and today he would perhaps even deny its possibility - *there would come a day when the old man too would hear the echoes of love and the promise of love coming back to him riding on the wings of love.*

The old man never seemed to know that the little boy was there but to little Joey that didn't matter. It didn't matter because *he knew that he sat there! And he knew why!* Somehow, the little boy knew that the old man was crying lonely tears and he knew that no one should cry lonely tears alone! And before he realized what was happening, the little guy was living the same sadness that the old man felt.

Chapter 40

THE WATCHER'S MISSION IS NOT ALWAYS EASY TO EXPLAIN

One of the things that humankind finds it difficult to explain is the extreme of things. For instance, to say that a light year is the number of miles that light travels in a year, which is almost 6 trillion miles, is easier to recite than is to cause some people to have a feel or sense of how far that is. Or to say that a nano second is one billionth of a second may fall short of actually causing someone to truly know the length of time of a nano second. Extremes often defy true defining because the untrained human mind is not always able to comprehend them.

The answer the question that Joey's mother asked, "Joey, why are you crying," is one such extreme. How does a boy who is only eight years of age express the reason for his tears when they are being shed in sympathy for another who, incidentally, he has never met? And how does he tie into the equation the fact of his sorrow over his little dog Sparky dying and why he feels responsible for the lonely tears that the old man is shedding? And how does he give account for him understanding the grief of the old gentleman? The answer is that the Master Watcher so designed the experience for the man and the boy.

The beautiful summer sun was going down. All of the children on her block were in their houses and the street looked deserted; like it did at about nine o' clock in the morning on a school day. Joey's mother knew that he would eat his supper when he came in so she hadn't called him in to eat when she ate earlier. But now it was getting late. The street lights would soon be on.

His mother called to him out of the back door and when he didn't answer she called up the stairs for him. When she couldn't find him anywhere she remembered that she had not seen him since he went to the park. Usually he came home long before this time. She started to panic and grabbed her jacket and dashed out the door to the garage. The park was only three blocks away but it was so much later than Joey usually came home and she knew that he was always such an obedient little boy. She jumped into her car and backed out of the garage and drove quickly toward the park.

When she got there she jumped out of the car, slammed the car door and ran across the street to the park. The only people she saw were two people who were sitting on a bench. One looked to be a child and the other one was larger than a child. She recognized the red and white shirt and she could tell by the way the little boy wore his baseball cap that the little kid was her Joey. But she could not tell who the other person was. She walked toward them until she heard the sound of them crying. She started running again. She ran to her son and said, "Joey, what is the matter? Why are you crying?" She quickly looked over his clothes and decided that he hadn't fallen down and hurt himself. And there were no signs that he had been in a fight with some other kid.

When Joey's mother found that Joey was not hurt, she calmed herself and began to talk in a whisper so she would not disturb the old man who was still quietly crying.

"What is the matter, Joey?" she whispered. She stooped down in front of the little guy so she could see him face to face. She saw that his little legs that were too short to reach the ground were trembling. She took him in her arms and held him close to her chest. The little boy had been crying so long that he could not stop right away.

"Son, please tell me why you are crying!" His mother pleaded. Joey looked up at his mother and took some deep breaths. He saw the worry on his mom's face and started blinking back his tears. His mother held him tighter until he was calm.

When he had caught his breath and could talk, he softly said to his mother, "Mom, I was over there sitting on the swing thinking about Sparky and I saw this man come into the park. You know that we have seen him here many times. But every time I saw him before today an old lady was with him. But, Mom, today he didn't look like *he was just by himself - he looked like he was by himself - all alone!*" She knew that Joey had always been a thoughtful and sensitive child but she never thought that he could feel and care as deeply as he cared today about this old man. She wished that his father was home from the war in Iran so he could feel the pride and the love that now flooded her heart.

CHAPTER 41

TEARS ARE CRIED AT ANY AGE

Our Almighty and Eternal Lord, Jesus, is Invulnerable to all attacks but feels the same pain we feel! Little Joey, though much younger than old Skeeter, feels the same pain that Skeeter feels! The was the Great Watcher's divine agenda all the time!

The evening was getting dark and a warm breeze was rustling the leaves of the old Oak tree. The lights had just started to come on in the park and his Mom knew that the street lights were also coming on.

Joey continued, "Mom, he looked all alone like I was the day that Sparky died. And when I saw him sit down where he and the nice lady had always sat together, I heard him crying and I looked at his face. He was so sad and was crying so hard. Mom, I remembered how tall he used to stand when that old lady leaned on his arm. And I remembered how he used to smile at her like he was so glad to be with her. But, today he looked like he was all broken inside and I wanted to help fix him. I remembered when I cried because of Sparky dying and how hurt and sad I was. And from the way that he was crying, I could tell that he had so much crying left to cry."

Joey looked into his mother's face with a look of confusion on his face and said, "Mom, while he was crying he reminded me of last winter when my Sunday school class was learning songs to sing on the Christmas program. I remember that we learned the song called, 'The First Noel'." Now his mother looked back at Joey with a confused look on her face.

"Why are you talking about the Christmas program, Joey?" she wondered.

Joey whispered, "Well, I might be wrong, but while he was crying I thought I heard him saying, 'Noel, Noel, Noel', over and over in between his breathing. Mom, I know that it's not Christmas so why was he saying, 'Noel?' Then his mother understood what Joey was too young to understand. The old man was grieving for his wife who must have just died. Joey's mother realized that his wife's name was 'Noel' and he wasn't thinking of a Christmas carol. He was calling his wife's name!

Joey's mother looked over to the old man who was still weeping and their eyes met. Old Skeeter had long ago accepted that he was a full grown man so his crying in the presence of a woman that he did not know did not embarrass him. Through his tears, the old man saw in her eyes an understanding and a knowing. But he saw more than that too. He saw a willingness to care and to help.

Skeeter didn't know the little boy who was sitting on the bench next to him nor did he know just when the little guy sat down. But what he did know was that when he became aware of Joey he felt less alone and less lonely in his crying. Little Joey had proven to Old Skeeter that there was still love in this world for him. He had reminded Skeeter that life is about caring and doing for others.

Joey's mother felt Joey tugging at her sleeve as she hugged him. She gave her attention back to Joey and asked him," Why were *you* crying, Joey? Were you still crying about Sparky?"

Joey looked at his mother and said, "At first I was thinking about how I missed Sparky." Then he pointed at Skeeter who was still sitting next to him at the far end of the bench. He was still very gently shaking but Joey could no longer hear the sound of his crying. "But when he came into the park and sat down, he was crying so hard! Mom, I could tell that his tears were too heavy for him and his pain wouldn't stop hurting him! And I remembered when my tears were heavy and my hurt wouldn't stop after Sparky died! I know how hard it is to have to push all of the hurt out through your eyes; though your tears!" Joey looked up at his mother with a look of fierce determination. She saw in him the strength of resolve to protect and to defend the weak; she saw the strength that real heroes are made of. She knew then that her Joey would always be a voice for those who had none and a defender for all who were too weak to protect themselves. And she knew that in the years to come many people would share in her pride of her son. It was a quality of true humility and selflessness that caused Joey to be unaware that he was doing anything loving, just and noble. He continued his explanation to his mother, "And I knew that he shouldn't have to do all the crying by his self. So when you came and saw me crying, Mom, *I was just <u>helping him cry</u>*.

CHAPTER 42

THE SPACES BETWEEN THE BARS

In the times that this story takes place, there was a real need for Watchers in the Negro community. Racial prejudice was rampant in America. If the Colored folk had no Watcher to intervene for them, the White folk often took advantage of them.

Tonight I was watching the news and because it is February and Black History month, one of the news stations had a piece about some of the terrible injustices that many Black people had suffered in the past. This got me to thinking about a story that my granddaddy had told me. It was a story that told me of my granddaddy's great strength of character and of the times and the culture that necessitated that strength. This all happened about fifty years ago.

It was very late on the night of my sixteenth birthday. Everybody had gone to bed except me and my eighty-two-year-old grandfather. My grandfather and I had this thing between us every Saturday night. We stayed up late and watched old Western movies on the TV. Actually, we used two televisions. The one on the bottom was an old Curtis Mathis

TV that had been sold by the Curtis Mathis Company; the company that bragged that it sold the most expensive TV on the market. But the price for the TV when it was new didn't bother Grandfather a bit because by the time Dad and Mom got it from Old Mr. Leroy, the junk man, the TV was already old. "Old Mr. Leroy, the junk man," that was what I always called him, I don't know why, but I always said, "Old Mr. Leroy, the junk man," when I talked about him. The TV, an old Motorola, sat on top of the old Curtis Mathis!

You see, the sound had long since played out on the Curtis Mathis but it still had a great picture and there was no picture on the Motorola any more but it had sound. So, we heard the sound from the Motorola and saw the picture on the Curtis Mathis TV.

You know, I can see the whole scene now almost just as if I was there in the living room of that old clapboard house of too many colors. The heavy rains in the spring, the hot sun in the summer and the blistering cold of the Detroit winters had peeled the paint off the house so badly that probably every color that the house had ever been was seen barely hanging on. That was the outside of the house. In the living room, I can see the old oil stove that Dad and Mom had bought brand new to replace the old potbellied stove that sometimes glowed a deep red when I threw in too much wood! Then, there was the floor that Dad had covered with some old linoleum that Grandfather got from Old Mr. Leroy, the junk man. That must have been the coldest floor in town in the winter. When I woke up many mornings there was actually frost on the floor for about two feet out from below the windows!

I can see the old faded pictures that sat on the mantle and the lamp that hadn't worked in ages standing on the three legged table (it was made like that) in the corner next to the couch.

Some movie that starred Randolph Scott and Stoney Burke was on the TV at the time and Grandfather was really all into it! I was sitting there wondering just how I was going to ask Grandfather the question that had not left me alone for about nine or ten years. I'd heard my dad and Grandfather talking about it one day and when I asked Grandfather about it he told me that he would tell me all about it when I got to sixteen years old. Oh well, now I was sixteen and had been trying to find the right time and the right words all day long.

A few minutes ago I had decided that when the next commercial came on I would just come out with it! So, I did.

"Gandy, can I ask you a question?"

He tugged on one if his suspenders with one hand and rubbed his chin with the other and said, "Well, it must be a doozy of a question, Buddy, 'cause it's been a long time since you called me 'Gandy!' What's on your mind, son?" I used to call him 'Gandy' when I was small because I couldn't say "'Granddaddy.'"

"Gandy, you and Dad are the most honest men I know. It just never made sense to me that you would ever commit a crime! Do you remember when you said that you would tell me about when you were in prison once I turned sixteen? Well, I'm sixteen now!"

Granddaddy's chin dropped to his chest and with a deep sigh, he said softly, "I guess you've got to learn about things sooner or later! This is just as good a time as any." He seemed so sad at that moment that I thought that he must have really done something that he was ashamed about.

"It was when I had just turned eighteen, Buddy. I wanted to buy an old Ford car that a neighbor, Mr. Walt Jenkins, had for sale. So, I went to his house to talk to him about it. He said that he only wanted seventy-five dollars for it. But, that was a lot of money back in those days, son. And I didn't have it. Mr. Jenkins told me that he would give me all summer to earn the money but I had to have all of the money by the first of September. Now, that was just what I needed to hear. I had just gotten a job at the new restaurant over on McDougle Street. I was going to wash dishes and bus tables eight hours a day. I was going to make twelve dollars a week so I knew that I would have all of the money by the first of September."

Granddaddy shook his head hard as if he needed to loosen something in it that had been too long stuck in his brain and said, "Your Uncle Dan and your Uncle Ben warned me not to work for Mr. O'leary because they had worked for him in his old store. They both said that he either wasn't going to pay or he would keep promising to pay for weeks and even then he would cheat you. They said that Mr. O' Leary really loved money and he had a real strong hate and disrespect thing going for colored people. I even heard that one time he paid a wino a bottle of wine to beat up some little colored boy to get the little kid off his back. He owed the kid a paycheck.

He looked up at me to see if I was listening to him. I was listening so he continued, "I believed them, Buddy," Granddaddy continued, "because everybody was saying the same kind of thing to me about Mr. O'Leary. But I didn't - no, *I couldn't* let that stop me! I just had to buy that car! So,

I started working for him and just as soon as it was time for me to get my first pay he started in with the excuses! I was to be paid on Saturday night when we closed. But just like everybody had told me, Mr. O'Leary started in with the excuses right away!

"I'm not paying you until Monday because I got some unexpected expenses. I'll pay you Monday!" he promised. "He didn't apologize or anything. He acted like I had some nerve asking him for my pay! The look on his face kind of scared me so I hurried up an' got out of that restaurant!"

Granddaddy stopped talking and reached for his coffee cup with the picture of Fredrick Douglas on one side and Abraham Lincoln on the other. I knew that it was either going to be empty or it would be too cold! It was empty so he began again.

"And 'twas all downhill from there! At first, I kept working because he owed me. Then I kept working because he owed me so much that I couldn't bear to leave without getting something. Finally, I knew I had to talk to him about my money!"

Granddaddy squint his eyes like he was trying to see past me to that day so many years ago. He took out the red and white checkered handkerchief that he always had in his back pocket and wiped his face. I think he was just taking his time and focusing on this part of the story.

"Buddy, I'll never forget it! It was on a Tuesday, the day I had to clean the walk-in cooler. There were no customers in the place so I walked up to him. There were booths and there was also a long counter where people could eat and where the cash register was. That was where he always sat - by the cash register and his money."

"Um, Mister. O'Leary, I need my money today!" I think I shouted at him. Maybe I said it so hard and in such a stern voice because I being so scared, I had to force the words out. I don't know if he was angry because I hadn't asked him if I could speak to him or because he knew that I wanted to talk about getting my money. But the next thing I knew he was yelling at me and callin' me the "N" word! Then he had got up from his stool at the counter and was in my face yelling some more and spitting his garlic breath all up my nose! When I saw His fists balled up, I knew that he was about to hit me. You will never know how glad I was when the bell that was hanging over the door rang! Talking about an answer to prayer! This time God answered my prayer quick, fast and in a hurry! Somebody was coming in! I look around toward the door and saw that it was Mr. Wilson from the barber shop down the street! I was so hoping that someone would because I knew that Mr. O'Leary would back off if a custom came in! But when I saw who it was I wasn't sure that the cavalry had come and not just one more means old man! I couldn't be sure that anything would change now because I had one time heard the two of them talking about how too many "uppity Coloreds" were moving into the neighborhood!"

My Granddaddy paused to catch his breath or to figure out how to tell me this part without losing my respect. Granddaddy leaned back in his chair, rubbed his chin and went on with his story.

"By this time my anger had at last caught up with my fear and passed it right on by! I was so mad that I promised Mr. O'Leary, "I'm going to get my money one way or another!""

"You'll get nothin' from me and if I catch you around here ever again I'LL KILL YOU! YOU'RE FIRED! GET OUT OF HERE RIGHT NOW!" he yelled.

"I knew that I was never going to get my money now so I left and almost slammed the door off its hinges on the way out! Oh, I knew about prejudice and hatred but I never knew the depth that it could come from in the heart of a seasoned and veteran hater!"

"The next morning, I was sitting at home in the basement of our house fuming and seething over all that had taken place for most of the summer! I knew I had worked hard! I was never absent or late. I had even worked overtime in the hopes that mean old Mr. O'Leary would value my efforts and pay me what he owed! But he just took my willingness to please him for weakness. I know now that he was never going to pay me from the beginning!"

"All of a sudden, I heard the front door being kicked in! Then, I heard voices yelling my name! I ran upstairs to see what the commotion was all about! As I came through the cellar door, two big burly policemen were all over me! They threw me on the floor and almost broke my arms as they twisted them around my back to put handcuffs on me!"

"You are under arrest for the burglary of Fine foods restaurant!" one of them told me.

"I didn't understand what had happened! I had heard of this kind of thing occurring but NOT TO ME! This happened to strangers on the TV news and in the papers! So much of the rest of the story seems even now to be a big blur! It was all over the TV. 'David Tolbert arrested for burglary of the Fine Foods restaurant. $6,538.00 was allegedly stolen!' "To let that stingy, greedy man tell it when I was asking for my money, he never even had $600.00. Now, he was saying that I had stolen over $6,000.00! The big racist liar!

"Well, they had their trial. My family, friends and even teachers from the Colored school I had graduated from testified of my good character but when those twelve men, good and true, who sat on that jury heard Mr. Wilson testify that he heard me say I was going to get my money "one way or another," I knew I was sunk! I knew it just as sure as I knew Mr. O'Leary was a racist and a thief! They gave me five years in the State penitentiary."

Granddaddy pulled what was left of an old ottoman closer to him and propped his feet up. "Buddy, will you open the window and put the stick under it for support? I'm kinda hot now," Granddaddy said. I got up and walked over to the window!

When I looked out the window, I couldn't help wondering how far removed from those days and those happenings we were now so many years later. Has much changed since then? How much danger am I in today from the guile and the wiles of mean and hateful racists?

Looking out of that window, I remembered one day when I was only nine years old and my mom was in the kitchen washing dishes. I was in the living room lying on the floor reading the funnies. I read the funnies every day. I saw a picture on one of the pages that showed a boy that looked to be about ten years old, the same age as me. The picture showed a big white police officer siccing a big German shepherd dog on the kid. The words under the picture just gave an explanation about why the dog had *not* bitten him. The boy was leaning back on one foot while he had his other leg lifted up with his knee warding the dog off. The caption read, "My Dad told me that if a dog attacks me just keep him away with my knee to his chest." I always thought that there was something wrong with that! I felt that something should be said about how many kinds of wrongs it was for the big policeman to make his dog jump on that little kid.

I was so bothered by that picture and what it said that I went into the kitchen where my mother was washing the breakfast dishes. I can see her now standing at the sink with suds on both hands, her hair combed back in the familiar bun that was her everyday style. She had on the yellow dress with the sunflowers that I had seen her wear for umpteen times! On her feet were the now, old, house slippers that me and my older brother, Jay, had given her for mother's day last year.

"Mom," I blurted out, "Do white people "down South" like black dogs?

I didn't have a clue where "down South" was. It could have been in another country for as much as I knew. Also, you must know that I must have certainly been bothered by that picture because if I had been thinking straight, there is no way that I would have used the term, "White" people! My Dad and Mom would have pitched a fit if I had! Mom used to say, "Do you know how thin that person's skin is? He is much more than the color of his skin! He is a man! He is more than a "White" man! When you call him a "White man, you are adding up all that he is and coming up with a color! That is all kinds of wrong!" She didn't even want us saying, "That Colored man." A man truly is so much more than the color of his skin! I could describe the clothes he was wearing, the kind of work he does and I could have even told what kind of car he drives! But I could never describe him by the color of his skin!

Anyhow, I guess this thing had gotten to me so much that I forgot the "White skin" rule! Well, when my Mom heard my question, I guess she forgot the rule too because she completely ignored it!

"Yes, Buddy, they do." she replied.

"Do they like brown dogs?

"Yes, child," Mom said.

"Do they like white dogs?"

"Of course they do, Buddy. She answered. "Now, what is this all about?"

I lifted the newspaper article and showed her what I had just seen. She then spoke in her low, quiet voice that said that she was thinking about something serious. The look on her face was the same look that she had when she had something on her mind; something she use to say, "...Won't leave me alone!" The look that this time said that *something had made her very sad!*

It seemed that her hands had frozen in the dish water! She looked down at the dish water for a long moment, and then she slowly turned her head to look down at me! As she was turning to look at me I saw what I have seen only a few times in my life because my Mom was a very strong, back then, "Colored," woman! I can see even today, the tears that slowly glided down her face, glistening and building and gathering in intensity! Seeming to ignore my face but looking directly into my eyes, she instructed, "Buddy, we've just got to pray!" She said it in that same quiet voice.

It was ten years later, when I had come home from my first leave after basic training, that something (I don't remember what) triggered the remembrance of that episode in my life. I waited until me and Mom were alone and reminded her of that incident. Of course, she remembered it!

"Mom, there is something that I have wanted to ask you *about that day* for a long time. But I didn't know how because you were so terribly affected at the time it happened!"

"Well, what is it, Son," Mom wondered. "You can ask me anything! I can take it! I'm sure I have endured worse things in my life time!"

Looking into her face this time, I wanted to be sure that I didn't make her weep again. I asked, "Mom, why did you cry that day?"

Again, Mom seemed to ignore my face and looked straight into my eyes and said, "I realized that you were becoming aware of the world around you and at such a young age and in such a harsh way! I knew that you were losing your innocence, son, and therefore much of your childhood! I knew also that you can never go back once you walk away or as in your case are driven away from your innocence! I wasn't ready to lose my boy yet. I knew that it must happen for that is the way of life. But not this way, Buddy! Not at this time! I was simply mourning the loss of my little baby boy."

You know, it's funny how the mind can work! All that I knew in remembrance took seconds to relive. I knew that my Granddaddy always wanted me to do what he said right away and not "dawdle," (as he called it when I was too slow to do what he told me to) so, I hastened to raise the window and prop it up.

"You know," Granddaddy continued, "I guess it was sometime in July of the fifth year that I was locked up when the guy that shared my cell asked me a question. Apparently, he had been watching me for a long time. Finally, he just came out with it!"

"Tolbert, why do you keep *staring at those bars* in the cell window every day, most of the whole day long? You must think that you can wish them away or something! Man! They ain't goin' nowhere until your sentence is up! Why don't you make this easier on yourself and just accept that you are here and ain't gon' leave no time soon! Stop fightin' it! You are in the Joint! You are locked up! You are incarcerated! So, just sit down and do your time!"

Granddaddy paused for a moment, as if he had just stepped out and away from me and was back in that terrible place of his imprisonment! His eyes had a kind of look that said he wasn't seeing me, the living room or anything of today. I had the feeling that he knew that he was talking to me but it seemed that he was talking more *at me than to me!* Then he said in a voice low and husky, "I told that youngster that he ought to mind his own business because, first of all, he didn't know me! So he didn't have a clue as to what was going in my mind! Secondly, He really must not know very much about my God, because years ago…. Buddy, look at me, Boy!" He barked.

My eyes were closed as I was trying to picture that cell; see that cellmate and see that day. When Granddaddy called me, I opened my eyes and saw him hitting his knee with his first finger in a gesture that was patently his, meaning, "*Don't you miss this!*"

"I truly gave my life to my Savior, Jesus Christ," he went on, "and that was the true beginning of any wisdom that I might have today! One of the many things that my Lord taught me is that for every obstacle that man, beast or demon throws in my way, God places at least one and probably more avenues of escape or means to safely and efficiently deal with it! For every "No" man gives that restricts me, God provides a "Yes" that frees me! As a matter of fact, He made me to know beyond any shadow of a doubt that He will never tell me "No" unless He has a better "Yes!"

"So, I let that youngster know that I was not staring *at the bars! I was too busy ignoring them!* You see, Son, the young man was incarcerated in a way that I never was! When he looked at the cell doors and windows, he saw what I refused to make my focus! He saw the smallest elements in the construction of the jail doors and windows! I was staring at something that was larger and more promising than the bars! Because he was jailed in his mind, he had no true awareness of anything but the objects of his confinement; the bars! Yes, I had to let him know that I was not staring *at the bars!* I was staring at *the spaces between the bars!* I let him know that if I focused on the bars than I would indeed be *"In the joint; locked up and incarcerated!* But, when I focused on *the spaces between the bars,* I could go home and enjoy the company of my beloved wife and daughter or play with my son or go to church and worship with those who know, trust and love me! *The spaces between the bars* allowed me to go wherever I long to be at any given moment! I let that know-it-all youngster know that in *the spaces between the bars I was a free man!*"

"Son, God made me to know that *you cannot bind a man whose mind is free!* You've got to realize, Buddy, there was power *in the spaces between the bars!* Listen to me good, son! Man made the bars but *God made the spaces!* Man made those bars to work against me while *God made the spaces between the bars to work for me!* For every restriction and constraint, for every negative and pain that the man- made bars cursed me with, *the spaces between the bars provided* me with a liberty and a freedom and positive sources of joy that the designers of the prison never intended for me to have!"

"Get this Buddy," he continued, "everything that man makes is filled with flaws and weakness because man's designs are not perfect! Those bars were strong enough to keep my body bound but they also, by God's design, created the spaces! Should there have been no bars because the door was a solid piece of steel, perhaps all that I would have perceived would have been the hopelessness and the blackness of an abysmal and bottomless depth! And if there had been only an abyss that was full of the emptiness and fruitlessness of despair; if there had been only an abyss that would have swallowed up all of my joys, my dreams, my visions, and ultimately my loves for which I truly live; I don't know that could have survived my prison term! Or what if the door had simply been built with a large opening where the bars should have been? *That large opening;* would have had to somehow offer restriction and incarceration because it was, after all, a prison. *That large space* would of necessity have to provide the constraints which would make all that I was yearning for seem so far away and so impossible to attain! Maybe all I would have seen in that tantalizing and teasing *space* would have been such a "cruel and unusual punishment" that my heart could not have borne its weight! Perhaps, I could not have endured!"

"Buddy," he continued as he looked directly into my eyes, holding my gaze, "I could not prevent them from enslaving my body but my God made me to know that my mind was not their's to control! That is why my God taught me to see only *"The Spaces Between the Bars!"*

CHAPTER 43

I KNOW YOU HAVE MY BACK - I STILL FEEL THE

Knife You Left There!

All too often it may be discovered that the same one who promised, "I've got your back," really had your back! The proof is the knife they left there! But the knife wasn't left because no one was Watching! Rather, the Master Watcher not only saw it all but knew the hearts of those in this story and used their natural inclinations to accomplish divine Will!

Her back was against the howling wind. The gale played hard tag with the forgotten neck scarf that slapped her in the face! The unseen force whipped the scarf into a frenzy that caused it to appear demon crazed!

The young woman was kneeling. Her dark silhouette seemed to complete the shadowy tapestry blending of black, white and gray. The scene brought to mind the words, lonely, forlorn and forgotten. Her posture suggested something worse than surrender – it implied defeat. Her mien and carriage spoke of worse than consent – it expressed enslavement. She seemed to be in a kind of sad, cold and lonely agreement with the bleak wintry evening.

Influenced by the biting and cutting breath of the chilling winds, wooden, thrashing arms of leafless trees rattled against one another, seeming to slice at non-existent foes. Or perhaps their target was the very same mindless winds that pulled and dragged at the naked branches. The winds forced their way through the branches of the snow-powdered trees. Tacit sentinels, they were, standing latent, faking their own death - these trees. Sadly, they were the only witnesses to this sad drama.

The grave marker was an eerie whitish blue in the nocturnal cast of the moon's cold light. The figure of the woman kneeling in front of the tombstone was so small and still. Closer inspection would reveal, however, that the woman was not motionless at all. Rather, the moving shadows of wind, pushed clouds and the relentless agitation of trees and bushes around her, gave rise to the notion that she was motionless. She was, in fact, gently shaking with grief! Her whispered sobs could not be heard above the moaning of the winds. But no one was there to hear anyway - and she was beyond caring that no one cared.

Her name was Vivian Stone. Vivian was the most fitting name for her, according to her father who was a professor of literature. He would inform anyone who would listen that she was the most active baby that he'd had the pleasure of knowing! And the name, Vivian, is, after all, Latin for *lively*. She grew up as the only child of the parents who had brought her into the world when they were in their late forties.

Perhaps it was because they knew that they would never have another child that they showered her with toys, clothes, trips and everything else they thought she would enjoy. However, despite all that they gave her, including all of the love she needed, in Vivian's heart, there was secretly always something missing. Her parents never knew how much *she wanted a sister!* She was never greedy and seldom asked for anything. This was partly because her parents always seemed to anticipate her desires and satisfy them and partly because she was so appreciative of all that they gave her that she never wanted her parents to feel that she was covetous and materialistic. Vivian could not remember a time in her life when she did not feel empty and unfulfilled when she thought of how badly she wanted a sister.

One of the reasons that she was able to love her husband, Leon, was that he loved children and wanted to have them as much as she did. They had lain awake in their bed many nights talking, planning and dreaming of the children that they knew would someday be born. They had even named them and decided, in their dreaming, the kinds of children they would be.

At the moment, on that cold day, in that colder cemetery, Vivian did not know whether her pain was greater because she lost her baby daughter, Willow, through a childhood sickness or because Miriam, her best friend, had betrayed her. Maybe the problem was made worse by the realization that it was through her best Miriam's betrayal *that she had been set up to lose her only child.* But did it really matter? Her baby, her little Willow, was dead and Miriam, her best friend, was dead to her! *And it was she who had lost them both!*

First, Vivian felt that she had been betrayed in the meanest, most vicious and heartless way possible! And secondly, just this past week Miriam had died and Vivian never had the chance to vent and tell her just what she thought of her! There had been no closure! Even though Miriam had died, Vivian felt that she had committed her heinous crime and had gotten clean away! "Because," Vivian reasoned, "Someday, Miriam was going to die anyway!"

You see, Miriam's husband, Archie, had been known to drive much too fast! For some reason, he felt that he could handle his car so well that nothing could ever happen to them *if he was driving*. Well, one evening Miriam and Archie were driving home and Archie wanted to get home in time to see the final game of the NBA playoffs. He knew that he was running late and was somewhat angry at Miriam for taking so long with the grocery shopping. All these things just resulted in him driving way too fast! He did handle the car well but no amount of driving skill could have saved them when they headed into that curve doing fifty-five miles an hour! The curve was in a thirty- five miles an hour speed zone. Both front tires blew and they went into a skid and careened into a tree! They both died instantly. Fortunately, none of their children were in the car.

It seemed so strange to Vivian that as great as her love had been for Miriam, her hurt, anger and disappointment were now so intense that all of her good feelings for Miriam were destroyed. Her anger was white hot!

Miriam had known more than anyone how much she wanted, no, needed a baby. Had it been anyone but Miriam who used her she believed she could have borne it. But Miriam misused and abused her! Miriam betrayed her and that she could never forgive!

She could not stop her mind from its insistent efforts to go back in time. Against her better judgment - and because she was so tired of fighting; she gave in to the mental shadows that would not be denied. She had known at the outset of her urge that she wouldn't really fight it for long. She now was desperate to see again what she never wanted to see in the first place. She felt a sudden lifting of weight and a great relief as she finally and completely gave in. The mental pictures began to form and the images finally became clear in her mind's eye. Vivian tried to prepare herself for the pain that she was certainly going to experience as she revisited both her earthly heaven and her earthly hell. The sudden explosion of joyful expectation that she couldn't help but feel at the prospect of reliving those precious moments, fought hard against a feeling of apprehension. How could the same images bring forth joy and sorrow, pain and ecstasy?

In her mind's eye, the scene shifted to that fateful morning she had talked to Miriam and told her she was coming over. Vivian had known before she went to her that whatever Miriam wanted she would probably give her. But now, as she considered her decision, she wondered if it was really hers to make! Miriam would listen to people very carefully to find any weakness in their arguments and then pounce on that weakness and manipulate it until she got what she wanted. And when all reason failed, Miriam would simple turn on her charm and people usually gave in. Vivian knew that Miriam could make herself appear so vulnerable and powerless that Vivian would never hurt her by denying her.

Nobody was there to see her icy breath puff in small clouds from her mouth, as she knelt in that cold and bleak cemetery. She never realized that her healing process would include *facing the cause of her pain!* She let her mind go where it was headed all the time.

She saw the scene shift to that fateful morning she had talked to Miriam at Miriam's request. Vivian saw the sprawling, white house out in the country where she had grownup. Feeling the familiar joy of being back home, she was comforted as she always was at the memory of the large porch that extended around the house on two sides. She imagined Miriam and herself on the porch in the shade of the great Elm tree that had been there long before she had been born. Miriam had come up on the porch and sat down next to her. After they talked for about twenty minutes, the pouting of Miriam's lips, coupled with the tears that were welling up in her eyes, was already breaking down Miriam's resistance. "If …if you take one of the twins and I take the other, the girls will still be together!" argued Miriam. You know we'll always be best friends!"

Miriam was talking in the way that was truly hers! She talked quickly and didn't let anyone else get a word in until she was sure her point was clearly understood. And Miriam could read her friend so well that she could tell that her point wasn't being received. She spread her hands expansively, indicating that she was being completely honest and sincere. "Look, girlfriend, my Archie says we can't afford two children and their mother wants the girls to stay together. But, I think she will let each of us adopt one of them because we are so close to each other. I mean, you know you are my very best friend in the whole world!"

"But have you seen them? And *are they healthy?*"

"Yeah, Girl, they are the two most beautiful babies I have ever seen! They look just alike except that one is a little bigger than the other. And the one that will be yours, even has a pert little turned up nose with some tiny little freckles just like you have!"

Vivian had a fleeting thought that something was wrong because Miriam wouldn't look at her when she said the babies were healthy. And only now did Vivian realize that Miriam had never answered concerning the health of the babies. Instead, Miriam had talked ever faster telling her how beautiful the babies were. Now, she understood why Miriam had avoided the question. Miriam had known *then that one of those babies was terminally ill <u>with only a few months to live!</u>* And <u>*she knew just which one it was*</u>!

Then, Miriam really turned on her sweetness, calling her, "Baby Girl," though she was only one year older then Vivian. Miriam always called Vivian "Baby Girl" when she really wanted something! "Remember, *this is not for me as much as it is for you* because the doctor says that <u>*Archie and I can have a baby.*</u> It's because I love you so much that I want you to have the sister to the twin that I will have! Baby Girl, I really want you to have this other twin and if you say, 'No,' I just don't know what I'll do!"

A Watcher who is true to the Watch will hold all aspects of the Watch in the highest regard! The <u>faithful friend</u> will never Watch having ulterior motives and will never place self above the treasured friend! Miriam is proving to be a true "Watcher" but <u>for whom is she Watching?</u> Be kindly affectioned one to another with brotherly love; in honour preferring one another...." Rom 12:10

CHAPTER 44

YOU CAN HAVE A NEED THAT YOU MORE THAN NEED

True "Watching is usually multi-layered! It is as if God gives safety nets in case a "Watcher" fails to prove faithful! Most assuredly, Miriam is the Watcher for someone! And while Miriam is proving to be selfish, God has another "Watcher" who truly loves Miriam!

Vivian remembered asking herself at the time of the discussion why Miriam and Archie really wanted to adopt if they could have had their own baby. But Miriam hadn't given her anytime to pose the question. She had just kept talking until she had gotten the answer she wanted!

Though the air in the cemetery was getting more and more frigid, Vivian seemed completely oblivious to the change, so given was she to her tortured daydream. She didn't realize that her knees had become numb as she knelt before the headstone. Nor was she aware of the powdery snowflakes that were now swirling around her.

Slowly, as the hopeless mind is apt to do, her thoughts seemed to focus on the new images that were forcing her to pay attention to them. She was no longer seeing herself and Miriam on the porch at her house. Rather, in her dream state, she saw herself and her husband riding in their car on the way home from the hospital. The change was so gradual; so incremental that she was not even aware that she was seeing a new scene. She watched an earlier drama unfold before her.

"Oh, Honey, I have never been so disappointed in my life!" she recalled herself sobbing. "I just knew that some way, somehow, something would happen and our dream would come true! This is the second doctor that we've seen. I was hoping so hard that he would say something else – something positive! I was so sure that somehow he would say I can have a child!"

"I know, Baby, I was hoping too," her husband, Shawn replied. "But, I tried to get you to not get your hopes up too much!"

Vivian remembered getting quiet as she debated whether to tell him about Miriam's plan. "What would he say?" she wondered.

She knew Shawn didn't approve of Miriam. He believed she was sneaky and conniving. He was often known to say, "That woman is as crooked as a dog's hind leg! She doesn't care for anyone but herself!"

But why couldn't he see any of the qualities that made her a good friend? Miriam made everyone laugh no matter what they were going through. She and Miriam had met in their freshman year of high school and they had been close friends ever since.

Vivian remembered how her need for a child had won out despite her doubts. "Sweetheart," she began, "Miriam knows a woman who has twin girls. She is not married and her boyfriend won't take any responsibility for them. Besides, she has three children already and truly can't afford any more."

"But, Baby, you know we're talking about what *Miriam* says," he reasoned. "Since when can we believe *anything* that comes out of her mouth?"

She knew that her husband was not alone in his opinion about Miriam. That was the reason that Miriam hadn't many friends. Few people trusted her! She closed her eyes and tried to swallow a lump that would not go down. Her eyes stung from the hot tears that were brimming beneath her eyelids. In a voice that was hardly a sound at all; it was almost as silent as a thought, she whispered with all of the passion she felt in her too full heart, "Please, Honey, I really want one of those baby girls more than I've ever wanted anything! It's just like when I wanted so hard and so much for you to ask me to marry you!" she explained.

The terrible pain in her heart could not be hidden or mistaken. She had known her husband could not deny his wife whom he loved so much. Nor could he say that he didn't want the opportunity to adopt this baby. The truth is he wanted to be a father as much as she wanted to be a mother!

Quite often both the "Watcher" and the "Watched" have similar interests and desires! No one will care about your treasure more than someone who treasures the same thing you place great value on! This woman's husband loved her and he loved what she loved! "For where your treasure is, there will your heart be also." Matt 6:21 KJV

CHAPTER 45

VIVIAN HAD A NEED AND SHE WAS THE NEED HER BABY HAD

"A friend loveth at all times, and a brother is born for adversity." Prov. 17:17

The need to "Watch" may be as great in the "Watcher" as the need to be "Watched" is to the unprotected and vulnerable. The ever loving "friend," and the faithful "brother" who is "...born for adversity" are empowered to live their lives to the fullest. They know and have embraced the purpose that Divine Order has determined is the reason and meaning for their existences. They can live contented and rewarding lives!

Kneeling in the icy cold, Vivian couldn't stop the hot tears that burned her cheeks despite the cold wind. She remembered seeing her little girl for the first time. The baby girl *seemed to be a perfect little doll!* Her hazel eyes and curly dark brown hair were beautifully complemented by a complexion that the older folk called, "high yellow." Her bright hazel eyes gave meaning to the old saying, *"The eyes are the windows of the soul."* Looking into those eyes, as she remembered, she could see the essence of innocence, the image of purity. She could recognize a promise of joy and delight too perfect to describe. This joy gripped her in the deepest recesses of her heart when she heard the first gentle cry of the tiniest, most wonderful gift she had ever received.

Willow was so small, so helpless. Her size only accentuated Willow's defenselessness which seemed to cry out to the woman. This same helplessness and need promised to fill a void of need in Vivian that was beyond resisting! Yes, Vivian had as much a need as the baby had! But, she never dreamed that her perfect little baby girl was really so sick!

From the first time she held Willow in her arms, Vivian knew the child was born for her! Her heart went out to the baby in a way that she had never loved anything or anyone before! By the time the doctors explained to her how sick the little child was - nothing would cause her to reject her child! Willow filled her heart with joy and her mind with the comfort of being needed and all her thoughts with cheerful hope for the future.

The biting cold was cutting deeper, nudging her away from the time of the happiest memories of her life - back to the hell of her present day. The howling winds and the clacking sound of the naked branches pulled her back to the reality of the moment. She sobbed, wondering again how the source of such exquisite joy could have brought such great sorrow. She knew she would never get over this misery.

As the winter froze everything around her, Vivian thought, "This is unconscionable! This is beyond forgiving! Miriam knew all the time how sick my little angel was! And Miriam knew how much I needed a baby! How could she be so cruel?"

Miriam really wanted to get a baby for herself! It didn't bother her that her best friend would know nothing but pain! Miriam didn't care about the terrible price that another was destined to pay so that Miriam could have her own baby!

Vivian, who was as beautiful in her grief and sorrow as she was in the days of her smiling, found herself wondering once again what she had done to deserve such misery. Though she never felt that she merited the beauty and fulfillment of life that her little girl had given her - she certainly knew she had done nothing to deserve to be punished *this way; this much*!

The utter futility of it all struck a dissonant chord in her mind. "What was it all for?" she whispered. "In what kind of mad game of human-heart manipulation was she an unwitting and helpless pawn? Had God simply allowed the devil to make sport of her? Or was God Himself playing some sort of divine chess game with her heart, her feelings?"

Her questions were harder still to deal with because years before, she had given her life to Jesus Christ - *to be safe, to be hidden in the refuge of His Love*! She had trusted Him with her life and her heart.

"Why did You let this happened to me?" She asked Him. "How could You have failed me this way?"

Even as these thoughts filled her consciousness, she knew that there had to be more to her suffering than she could readily see. The guilt and the shame that came to her were both immediate and undeniable. As a young Christian she had decided that she trusted her Lord not because <u>she knew what He was doing</u> *but because she was sure that <u>He knew what He was doing</u>*. Remembering this commitment, the woman fought hard to gain a spiritual footing in the quaking, shaking turmoil that threatened to destroy her faith and her Christian foundation.

In His own unique and altogether inimitable fashion, the Comfort of Her Soul gently began to reassure her with one of her favorite passages of scripture. She seemed to hear Him whisper to her heart from Proverb 3:5, *"Trust in the LORD with all thine heart; and lean not unto thine own understanding."* Then she remembered that He had promised her in Romans 8:28, "... *all things work together for good to them that love God, to them who are the called according to his purpose."* Then, to her wonder and amazement she felt the revival of a familiar calm and an abiding assurance. Somewhere in the deep divide between her heart and her soul another song began to be sung; another and a familiar Voice was heard. "I love you, My child, with all of My eternal heart! I am totally devoted to you. More than even you could ever love your daughter - I love you! *Just* trust me! *Purely Trust* Me! *ONLY TRUST ME!*"

At that moment her heart was filled with a trusting love! Her new found peace and assurance completely healed her pain and eclipsed her doubts. Before she realized what she was doing, her mouth opened and she broke into the harsh stillness of the cold cemetery with a praise that was on fire; a praise and worship that had its origin in the very heart of the Living God!

From the deepest recesses of her heart, the woman declared to her Savior, "I never knew You to be cruel and I know that some way even this will turn to my good!"

Then, in the periphery of her hearing, a sound invaded her mind. It was the insistent blaring of an automobile horn!

She heard a car door slam shut. Now someone was calling her name. She turned around and saw Shawn running toward her!

"I knew I would find you here!" he exclaimed. He took her by her hands and lifted her and then took her into his arms. She found sudden warmth in his embrace. The thought that her husband was just the right height for her to fit snug in his arms with her head just under his chin was contrasting with the issue of the moment! But it was a familiar observation for Vivian! She always felt that they were a perfectly matched pair when he held her in his arms.

As she leaned against him, she heard him say, "I have something to tell you."

With a heart filled with hope, she looked up at her husband and was stirred by the excitement and joy in his voice.

"You know that last week Miriam and her husband were killed in an automobile accident. But what neither of us knew was that when they adopted their child they made out a will! In the will they asked you and me to adopt their baby girl, the other twin!"

Suddenly, she understood! The Omniscient and Loving God wanted the sickly little twin to have the best love and care possible for the few months she would live! The Lord knew that Miriam and her husband were going to die and He arranged for the other twin to the raised by the mother who wanted a child *for the child's sake!* Miriam had wanted the baby girl so that Miriam could be happy! God knew the best mother would be the one who would want the baby *so that she could make the baby happy for all of the baby's life!*

The young woman could hardly endure the happiness that flooded her mind at what she was hearing! Oh, the joy that cascaded over her soul! She should have known that God would never let her down! Now she understood that she was never alone! She would never be forsaken or abused by her Savior. Now she could forgive Miriam - *for God was in it from the beginning!* The love of God had provided Miriam with a little girl to love for Miriam's few remaining days! Vivian finally got the whole pocture! God had so provided that Vivian and Shawn would have a little girl to treasure for all of her life!

You can be sure that if ever you find a knife in your back the damage need not be permanent! For, the Watcher's Watcher never sleeps or slumbers. He sees all and knows all <u>before it exists in our world.</u> And He uses all things to the benefit of His children.

What the young woman could not know is that the entire experience of loving and losing would only give her the capacity to love greater and more fully than ever she had love before.

How sad it is that many of God's Children have never learned how very much He loves them. God's love will never allow Him to say, "No," to those He loves unless the Grace of God has a better, "Yes!" God is so very concerned about every minute detail of our lives. We must trust God's love so much that we automatically know that God's "No" is better than our "Yes". Remember, God's peace is not satisfied in Him unless His Peace is completed in us.

Chapter 46

This is another excerpt from a series of essays that I've written through the years. I trust that you will find it informative, instructive, comforting and entertaining.

October 14, 2010

Basking in the Sun of the Son

It was a warm, almost tropical, morning in the middle of October. "My Brown Sugar" (my wife for the last forty-five years) and I were visiting my eldest son at his home in West Palm Beach, Florida along with my wife's brother, Virgil and his wife, Christina. I had determined the night before that I would go down to the beach to see the sun rise over the Atlantic Ocean. That morning my wife woke me up as I had requested her to do at around six o' clock. I got up and hurriedly dressed and prepared myself to go. Then I went down the elevator to the lobby of the hotel and requested a shuttle ride to the beach.

After about a five minutes ride I got out of the hotel shuttle and walked across the street to the sandy beach. The wind was blowing quite briskly from the east and the overcast sky was almost black with heavy bulbous clouds. I left the street, crossed the side walk and stepped into the warm sand. To my right and towards the ocean, I saw a cluster of rocks that seemed to be silent sentinels or at the least, soundless observers of a scene that had been played for countless years before this morning and was sure to be replayed, if man did not interfere, for untold millennia beyond this day.

While walking to the rocks, I found myself asking God for the umpteenth time why I had to come to Florida at this time in my life and despite the unsettled business that I had left at home in Texas. I approached the rocks and quickly decided which rock would be my seat. Climbing over some rocks and stepping between others, I tried to hurry to the largest and the flattest one before the next wave came in. Finally, I reached the rock that I had chosen and was surprise at its warmth after the strong winds of last night.

The sky was a dark blue and the last of the twinkling stars were giving way to the dawning of a new day. Already, the night birds were releasing possession of the wind and the sky to the birds that need their turn to ride those winds and bask in the light of the new day sun. I could see what appeared to be large dark holes in the sky between the thick clouds.

The sun began to make its entrance into the West Palm Beach morning and the sky that showed itself through the clouds changed color from dark blue to a lighter purple. Then the purple changed from mauve to a reddish orange. Eventually, I could see the promise of a glorious day because the clouds were fighting a losing battle with the brilliant shining of the sun.

Having seen the sun come up over the Ocean when my Brown Sugar and I were on a cruise in the Caribbean, I knew that (though it may take its time in coming) the sun will appear in the moment of a twinkling of an eye! When I reflected on this reality later, God emphasized to me the similarity between my waiting for the sunrise and my waiting for the Rapture of the Church.

The first comparison was in light of the timing of both occurrences. I didn't know just when the sun was going to rise but I knew that it would. I was encouraged to wait for the momentous event by the signs that heralded its soon appearance. Those signs were the wondrous metamorphosis of the sky; the wonderfully exquisite changes of colors before the sunlight exploded over the horizon with a tacit shout of victory and promise. It was as if the sun was simply trying to fill the night sky and the clouds with as much of its beauty and glory as it could but somehow it just went too far! It was as if it was so determined to end the darkness of the night that it just over achieved and its radiance broke through the obscurity of the night's blackness with a heavenly declaration that silently screamed to the world, "I, the Sun am here and a new day is begun! It is time to begin again to dream; to try again and this time to succeed! Today is the day you can win!" Sitting on that biggest of all of the rocks my heart sang and could not but break out in a smile that enveloped my face at the reassurances and the hope that spelled triumph over all.

Similarly, I know that the Rapture of the Church is going to come to pass! I have been waiting for the Coming of our Lord for more than forty-seven years now! Just as the changing sky gave life to my hope for the sunrise, the reality of God's Presence in my life and the signs that I and the rest of my Church family sees, keeps all of us ever looking up at the clouds with the greatest of expectations and the most real anticipation.

The Church has waited for almost two thousand years for the Second Coming of our Lord! However, in addition to the beautiful and wondrous signs that kept me believing and looking up to see the sunrise, the signs that the Church sees that keeps its hope alive are often mean circumstances. It is wars, rumors of wars with nations rising up against nations, earthquakes, pestilences, famines and the like that Jesus said would portend and foreshadow His Second Coming. The bottom line is - these signs give assurance and reassurance to true believers that the Rapture of the Church is the next significant and crucial event on Heaven's calendar.

Another comparison of the sunrise to the Rapture of the Church is that – just as the sunrise ushered in a new day, the Rapture will be the advent of a new eternity. The Rapture will be the initiation of a new day that will never end. And what a day that will be! Actually, the Rapture will be more than a new day for *it will be the initiation of the final eternity.* The Rapture will also happen "in the twinkling of an eye!" And in that moment, just as the sun rose in the sky, the Son of God will come down from Heaven. Just as the s-u-n rose with a shout of declaration of promise, so will the *S-o-n* come with a shout of promise.

(1Th 4:16) "For the Lord himself shall descend from heaven <u>with a shout</u>, with the voice of the archangel, and with the trump of God: and the dead in Christ shall rise first:

(1Th 4:1) Then we which are alive and remain shall be caught up together with them in the clouds, to meet the Lord in the air: and so shall we ever be with the Lord."

"I am the Son and I am Here!" He will proclaim. *"You have not simply won for today – you can never lose again! You never have to dream or try to succeed again. Because of Me you have won the Victory of all victories!"*

While *I sat on the rock* that was keeping me from the force and influences of the ocean water, I realized that *I was standing on "the Rock"* that has always been in my life to protect and defend me from the threatening waters and other ravages of life.

I remember so well becoming truly conscious of the foaming waves; the three feet high surf that came crashing upon the beach. For a few minutes, I sat there just looking at the water and listening to the sound of the nature of the sea as it played its role with the land. There was neither predictable rhythm nor cadence to the sound. The waters rolled on my right, my left and in front of me. The waves sometimes crashed together and at other times they seemed to race to be the first to hit the beach while at other times some waves seemed to lag behind. However, what was foreseeable was that the next wave was imminent.

The constancy of the ocean's motion was quickly reminiscent of the eternality of God. For a moment, I was struck with an understanding that seemed to move me physically, so strong was the impulse! I had no way of knowing just how long these waves had been beating against this shore; whether for hundreds of years; thousands of years or how many millennia. But I know that the same scene that I now witnessed had been happening for eons whether anyone was there to see it or not; whether any ears were listening to the sound of the surf or not. And I knew that long before there was an ocean or sand for its waves to wash up on – God was!

Eventually, I found myself looking at the cluster of rocks that surrounded the one I sat on. Then I took stock of the one that was my perch. I remember pressing down on the rock and feeling its firm hardness and density. I noticed that the rocks were very porous and abrasive. The thought came to me that it was the combined influence of the constantly rushing salt water and the sand that was caught up in the moving water that eroded the surface of the rock. Had this not occurred, the wet rock would probably have been too slick for me to climb it and sit safely and comfortably there.

Then I marveled again at how sometimes greatness is in the details. All that our Creator made He made so His masterpiece (man) would somehow benefit from it. It boggles my mind to think that millions of years before I ever sat on this rock on this beach, marveling at this sunrise, God knew I would. The Omniscient One saw me in the beginning and delighted *then* in the glory I would give Him on this day. Indeed, He made the sunrise, the ocean, the sandy beach and these rocks so that countless eons later I would have them to take pleasure in.

I don't know how much time past as I sat there musing and basking in the old and glorious sun of this new and splendid day. But in time, the love of God showed me a new reason to marvel at His genius. Next, He directed me to the pattern of the waves as the force that pushed them took them about twenty feet up on the sand. I watched them for a few minutes. The waves rushed up on the sand as if they didn't want to be late in the performance of their primordial duties and just as quickly they receded to the ocean leaving the sand dark and wet in their wake.

After viewing this for a few minutes, my Lord pointed me to some very small and very fat birds that were on the beach. These birds had very skinny and very tall legs. I wondered that the legs could hold their fat little bodies up. But they most certainly did and these birds moved very quickly across the sand.

At first I thought that God just wanted me to see the little birds run quickly across the beach but very quickly He made me to know that He had bigger fish to fry!

"Watch those birds!" He directed. So I watched the birds. I saw that when the waves came in the little birds did not move until the water got close enough to lap over their feet. This they did not allow to happen. The water came in from the ocean and when it got inches away from their feet the birds would take off running upland away from the ocean. They never ran completely away but stayed just close enough to the wave so that when the wave retreated back to the ocean, the little birds would quickly turn around and run back to the wet sand. Then they started pecking in the sand. God spoke to my spirit and said, *"When the waves cover the sand, completely hiding what was there and disturbing the peace of the beach"* He explained, *"it then goes back the way it came and back to where the water belongs. But the little birds are not disturbed by the disturbance of the sand because the waves leave blessings of food behind. It is the seeming chaos and disorder that*

is caused by the waves that provide the food that keeps the little birds fat."

I knew that there was now coming a revelation that would give life to this information and cause in me a transformation. So, I quietly waited for Him to continue.

"As you know that I love and care for the little birds, you must know that I love you and you must trust that love. No matter what chaos, confusion and disorder seems to wreck your world – trust that my love has provided the blessings that are sure to overtake you. Just wait out the time. The "waters" will recede to where they came from and I will leave blessings in their wake. You will then become fatter and more prosperous than you were before My "waves" covered your sand; more successful and affluent than you were when you were comforted by all that was your comfort zone and when you lived a life of predictable complacency. I promise that your patience shall be rewarded! You shall be wonderfully and exquisitely blessed!"

All this threatened to be too much to for me to take in at one setting but My Lord knows my capacity and my limits. So I sat there reveling in and delighting in the joy of my new realizations. I was most certainly aware of the fact that this episode of my life was most assuredly a pivotal turn in my understanding of my Heavenly Father. I was, further, aware with a most undeniable certainty that when I walked away from that beach I would be armed and strengthened with an assurance of faith in my Father, God, I have only longed to have before this day.

I knew to the greatest degree of certainty that I would not be bored this day. Speaking of boredom, while I heard the waves lapping and splashing against the rocks, I could hear the wisdom of God explaining a most profound truth to my spirit.

"When man is bored, it is because he has allowed himself to be so filled with himself that he has become the totality of the significant things of his world. It is then that his world is filled with a vast and so blank, emptiness. On the contrary, the man who is overflowing with an awareness of his own insignificance and his futility in comparison to the whole of creation and has learned to appreciate that the Omnipresence of God fills the world and that by Him all things subsists - then it is that man is fullest! Then it is that he knows the most exquisite quality of life imaginable! For, man is then saturated with the revelation that, in the grand scheme of things, man, in contrast to God, is nothing and - God is All!"

At some point, my focus was shifted to the waters of the Atlantic Ocean. As I gazed over the vast expanse of the ocean, looking as far as my eyes could see, I was most singularly struck with an abiding sense of the endless scope and range of both the Presence and the Power of God. That the water exists and has for untold eons stands as a testimony to the immutability of God's Presence and Power.

Slowly, as I enjoyed the salty spray on my cheeks, a thought began to take shape in my mind which was not a new thought at all but an idea revisited with a sharpness and a depth that I did not have until now! I have been conscious of the fact that since God first made the waters in the genesis of all things, He has never made any more water. I have known for some time that the same waters that the Father first made are the waters that we drink, bathe in and cook with today. This is true because there is very literally no place for water to go from this earth realm and no method for its complete and final removal. You see, water, when used or not, simply changes form from liquid to steam to liquid to ice to liquid to steam ad infinitum. I pondered this and I realized that this is not a new process. The same water that dinosaurs drank was the same water that refreshed Adam and Eve in the Garden of Eden. It was also the same waters that caused the great flood in the days of Noah and was the same water that John the Baptist baptized our Lord, Jesus Christ in eons ago! It is the same water that I dangled my feet in as I sat on this rock today! How awesome is our God!

While I sat there I began to appreciate what used to be simply the monotonous, repetitive and somewhat tedious motion of the ocean; the waves coming in and going out and coming in and going out again. I found that I was being filled with an overwhelming sense of my own security and my potentials in God. I have long known the scriptures that declare, "I can do all things through Christ who strengthens me" and "In Him we live we move and have our being." But on this day, I came face to face with the truth of those verses! I understood that the Word that God speaks is infused with all of the Power that our invariable and unwavering God is! That is why God's Word is constant and faithful! And that is why His Children continue to strive and are victorious against impossible odds!

The constancy and the faithful authenticity of the seascape included the sun in all of its brilliance; the beautiful azure waters, the sandy beach, the birds and indeed all that was my world at that time, on that day. All that my awestruck eyes took in pronounced to me in a stentorian voice that the words God spoke in the beginning of time are still alive today! Experiencing these wonders, I knew with a depth of understanding that heretofore was beyond my ability to comprehend, that His spoken words are still influential! They are still supplying the power and the directives that continue the life of His divinely spoken ordination.

It was then that I felt, even as I saw, the light of the sun. As I experienced the sun in these two dimensions, my Father gently reminded me that His infallible Word is the power that keeps the sun burning and producing light. Because, when God said, "Let there be light," He set in motion a law. Actually, what He literally said was, *"Let there be light, light, light, light,"* to the end of time. Since God said, *"Let there be light,"* there has been light somewhere on earth. All of this demonstrates with copious clarity the faithfulness of God and solidifies, in my heart, the certainty and the surety of my future.

When God saturated my mind and my spirit with these truths He capped it off by clarifying another truth. He taught me that the aspect of God's love that causes His children to have faith in Him is His Faithfulness! Because He had always been faithful – we can have faith in His Faithfulness!

I sat on that rock that day in the city of West Palm Beach Florida and wept. I wept for the promise that these truths gave me. I cried because of the tender touch of the masters Hand on my heart. I wept because He condescended to me, to one of such lowly estate. And I shed briny tears for the relief that was mine as He gave me a greater sense of purpose and a confidence in His Eternal Self as well as in my finite self.

By the time "My Brown Sugar" called me on her cell phone and interrupted my private reverie and musings, I knew that I had been raise to a loftier level than I had every before attained. I realized that I had transcended the height of understanding and the depth of expectation that was my life and my world. I knew beyond any doubt that because of the revelatory knowledge that so inexplicably and wonderfully reshaped my thinking, I was now standing on one world and looking quite expectantly into another.

When I climbed down from my rocky perch, I walked with a lighter step and with the spring of one who saw victory in his future. I walked with a purposeful stride and a glad song of an overcoming joy for I had truly basked in the "Sun of the Son of God!"